The Boojee Informants

A Thrilling Urban Fiction Novel That Will
Help You Succeed in Corporate America

Clean Version

The Boojee Informants

A Thrilling Urban Fiction Novel That Will
Help You Succeed in Corporate America

By Parker Wayde

Parker Wayde Publishing, LLC
Hillside, Illinois

The Boojee Informants
Published by:
Parker Wayde Publishing, LLC
Hillside, IL
info@boojeeinformant.com
www.boojeeinformant.com

Quality Press.Info, Production Coordinator
Creative Ankh, Interior Design
As it Seams, Cover Design

ALL RIGHTS RESERVED

No part of this book may be reproduced or transmitted in any form or by any means—electronic or mechanical, including photocopying, recording or by any information storage and retrieval system—without written permission from the authors, except for the inclusion of brief quotations in a review.

Parker Wayde Books are available at special discounts for bulk purchases, sales promotions, fund raising, or educational purposes. Contact: info@boojeeinformant.com

Copyright © 2013 by Parker Wayde Publishing, LLC
ISBN #: 978-0-9882178-2-9
Library of Congress Control # 2012921053

DEDICATION

To my people
I know how you feel
Just keep on pushin'
And make your dreams become real

ACKNOWLEDGEMENTS

BIG THANKS TO THE FAMILY AND
FRIENDS THAT LOVE ME.

PREFACE

I used all of my strength to try to pull my wrists apart but it was no use. The tape was wrapped around too tight and it wasn't budging. The blood from my wounded head mixed with sweat that was brought on by the intense heat that seemed to rise a degree with every second. I wiggled my toes, trying to increase the circulation that was cut off by the tape that bound my ankles, but it just seemed to make the pain in my numbing feet even worse. I tried to extend my legs but there was no room. I lay helpless inside the dark trunk of my own car.

I heard the engine of a vehicle pull into the parking lot and stop somewhere near my car.

"Help, help!" I screamed. "Somebody help!" This was my only chance to escape my kidnapper. I screamed louder but nobody came to my rescue.

BOOM! I heard a gunshot and the sound of tires screeching. The vehicle was moving fast and away from my car. BOOM, BOOM, BOOM!!! More shots rang out, but this time they ended with a loud, agonizing scream that seemed to last forever.

I sat silently waiting to hear what was next, now too scared to give away my location. Suddenly I heard footsteps coming toward me. The steps came closer and closer to the trunk. It was more than one person, more than two people... I couldn't count anymore. I closed my eyes as the trunk opened and the sun bounced off of the metal gun. My time was up.

SENIOR YEAR

OCTOBER 1991

ONE

Kandi

Ring. Ring. Ring.
I sat on the bed, holding the phone, waiting for Mitch to pick up.
Ring. Ring. Ring.
I slammed the phone down, madder than a motha.
"What's wrong girl?" Kim asked, putting on the last coat of her nail polish.
"Mitch's slow butt..." I mumbled.
I got up and paced the floor. Our room was as big as a kitchen pantry, so I wasn't going far. "He's supposed to give me a ride to dance practice but this fool won't pick up the phone."
"Maybe he's still at B-ball practice. You know he wouldn't stand you up like that, Kandi."
"Yea, whatever. Practice is over at seven. He should have been here by now."
Kim shrugged her shoulders and continued to carefully apply a glossy top coat to her big toe.
"Let me try him back. He better pick up the dangon phone."
I grabbed the phone and slammed my fingers against the keypad. *Ring. Ring. Ring.*
"Hello," a voice said on the other end.

I took the phone away from my ear and stared at the receiver. *Did I call the wrong number?*

"Hello?" the girl on the other end spoke again.

"Hello?" I said confused. "Is Mitch around?"

"Nope," the girl replied. "He's busy being with me. I can take a message and maybe he will get around to calling you back," the girl said, smacking her nasty big lips.

Kim saw my facial expression and jumped down from the top bunk, careful not to smear her pedicure. "Who is that?" she mouthed not making a sound.

I ignored Kim. I was trying to catch the voice.

"Who is this?" I asked.

"This is Sarah, who is this?" the girl asked with an attitude.

"Sarah, baby," I said calmly. "I'm glad you finally got a turn, I'm sure you waited in a long line, but tell Mitch that I better see him in 5 minutes." Sarah tried to reply but I slammed the phone down before she could finish the b-word that was half-way out of her mouth.

"Wait, what the heck was that!" Kim asked all revved up.

"Some wack groupie! Mitch better get it together. I ain't got the time!" I said steaming mad, tossing my gear into my gym bag. I stomped to the closet and grabbed my Betty Boop towel jacket.

"Where you going?" Kim asked.

"To practice. I don't need him to take me. I got two feet."

"All right," Kim said. "You want me to walk with you? I got to meet a study group at the library in 15 minutes…"

I cut Kim off. "Naw, I'm good. I'll meet you and Leon at the cafeteria when I get out."

"O.K. then," Kim said looking at me. She was examining my face to see if I was really O.K. She knew that I had a problem expressing my true feelings. I always had to be strong and tried to play it off no matter how much it bothered me.

"All right, peace," I said, grabbing the doorknob.

I probably looked half-crazy as I walked through the campus. I was mumbling to myself and kicking the crap out of every pebble that got in my way. There were so many things that I should have said to that stupid groupie. First of all, me and Mitch were just friends; naw scratch that, *best* friends. There was nothing going on between us, but for some reason I felt super disrespected. I couldn't believe that he would allow some lowlife to *one*, answer his phone, and *two*, talk to me like that. On the other hand, I didn't even know if I had a right to be mad. Like I said, we were just friends.

Beep, beep! A sound of a horn pulled me out of my own head as I walked past the entrance of the library. I looked over my shoulder and caught a glimpse of Mitch's car. He was riding on the shoulder, pacing along the side of me. I turned my head and kept walking. Mitch reached over to the passenger side and rolled down the window.

"Hey!" he yelled. "Why you walking? You want a ride?"

I kept walking.

"What's wrong, Kandi?" Mitch asked as if he really didn't know what the problem was. I rolled my eyes and continued to walk, "Punk." I mumbled. I had nothing to say to him and not even God Himself could get me to talk to him right now. Mitch hit the gas and turned the corner, cutting me off before I could cross the street. He threw the car in park and jumped out of the driver's side.

"Kandi," he said, walking toward me. "What's wrong with you girl?" He was now standing in front of me. I tried to keep walking but he grabbed my hand and pulled me toward him. "What's wrong, Kandi?" he asked searching my face for some sort of sign. I rolled my eyes.

"Well, I guess we gonna be out here all night long, 'cause I ain't letting you go until you tell me something."

"You want to know why I'm mad, Mitch?"

"Yea," he replied bucking his eyes and shaking his head.

I wondered if I should tell him. Did I even have a leg to stand on in this argument?

"Hello?" Mitch said awaiting my response.

Bump it, let it ride, I thought.

"Sarah is why I'm mad!" I yelled.

"Sarah?" Mitch questioned, looking even more confused.

"Yea, first of all, you was late picking me up, and when I called your tardy butt, Sarah, your boo, picked up the phone talking smack! What's that about Mitchell! I ain't one of your little hoochees!" I continued.

"Sarah," Mitch mumbled with his face all screwed up. Mitch

leaned back against the hood of the car and adjusted his letterman jacket so it wouldn't rub up against his father's old Beemer.

"Look man, I don't know how Sarah got in my room, but I was outside waiting on you. I was parked on the other side of the building and I didn't see you come outside. When I saw you cross the street, I came right over to scoop you up."

"Is that right?" I said sarcastically.

"Yea," Mitch replied.

I turned to walk away. Nothing is ever easy when it comes to me.

"Hey, hey, hey," Mitch said reaching for my elbow. "I'm for real, I wouldn't not come get you. You're on my favorite people list," he said, smiling. "I wouldn't let nobody bump their gums like that. I swear, I don't know how she got in my room."

"So, this is who needed to see you in 5 minutes!" I heard a familiar voice scream from behind me. I was so pissed that I didn't even hear anybody walk up on us. I turned around to face three girls standing behind me. The ringleader stood in front of the other two, her light-skinned face was glossy and full of Vaseline.

"Sarah!" Mitch yelled. "Get your crazy butt out of here!"

Mitch tried to pull my arm to pull me back. He wanted to shield me and stand in between the two of us, but I wasn't going. I snatched my arm from him and rushed the chick. We were chest to chest.

"Oh, you came for a fight, huh sweety!" I said landing my right fist against the girl's face.

"One on one!" I heard one of the other girls yell as they tried to surround us. She stumbled back from the force and tried to grab my pony tail but missed. She dropped her arms exposing her face so I popped her in the jaw.

"Kandi!" I heard Mitch yell. A crowd was starting to form. I could hear people yelling and rooting us on. Mitch finally got in between us, but Sarah just used the interruption as a way to grab ahold of my hair. I felt pain shoot across my scalp as my head violently jerked backward. I swung again, but she wasn't letting go.

"Let her hair go!" I heard Kim scream. "You got one more time, let her hair go!" Kim pushed through the crowd and slung her bookbag, hitting the girl upside her head. The force caused Sarah to loosen her grip. Both of Sarah's friends jumped in while Sarah stumbled from the dizziness. I turned my attention to help Kim fight off the other two hoodlums. Sarah recouped and jumped on my back. The extra weight caused me to go down. Mitch grabbed her by the waist, but not before she pulled her leg back to stomp me in the face. I braced myself for the hit. In a flash, a girl in a red jacket jumped over me and hit Sarah across the face. Both Mitch and Sarah fell backwards.

Whoop, Whoop. We heard the sirens in the distance and the crowd began to scatter.

"Get in the car!" Mitch yelled, grabbing the girl in the red jacket. Kim tugged on my hand and we all piled into the back of the Beemer as Mitch sped off from the corner.

"Can you believe that!" I yelled. Touching my face and looking at my fingers to see if I was bleeding. "Kim! You good?!" I yelled.

"Yea, she straight." The girl in the red jacket answered.

As we pulled up in front of the dance studio, the adrenaline began to wear off. The car got quiet as the three of us began to wonder the same thing.

"Umm, thanks, for umm helping us out." I said to the girl in the red jacket, trying to break the ice.

"It's cool, I don't like ole girl anyway, she took the last chocolate milk at breakfast today."

We all looked at each other and fell out laughing.

"They call me Ashley," the girl said holding out her hand.

"Well, it's nice to meet you Ashley. This is my friend Kim and..."

"Mitch," Ashley replied cutting me off. "Everybody knows Mitch. Good to meet you partner." Ashley held out her hand.

Mitch was reluctant to connect the hand shake, but did it anyway.

"Well, I'm about to run to practice real quick, but after this we are all going to meet up at the cafeteria. You think that you want to hang out with us later?" I asked.

"Sure," Ashley replied. "Just as long as y'all ain't no trouble makers."

I smiled at Ashley and giggled. "Naw man."

Ashley smiled back.

"I'll be there at ten."

"Cool," we all said in unison.

"Aye Ashley," Mitch yelled over his shoulder. "You need me to drop you off anywhere?"

"Naw, man," Ashley replied. "This is me right here."

We all turned and saw the shiny red sports car that was parked across the street.

"Yea, I'll see y'all at ten," Ashley said climbing out of the car.

We all sat and watched as Ashley unlocked the doors of the Porsche. She hopped in and started the engine. Ashley threw up the peace sign as she pounded on the gas and sped past us. We sat with our mouths wide open as we chucked it back.

Mitch

"Man, Leon, you should have seen it. I felt like I was watching a movie or something! There was hair pulling. Fists flying. People jumping on backs. It was crazy!"

Leon laughed as I re-enacted the scene. I ran up on a lonely looking freshman, just like Kandi did Sarah. The freshman looked like he was going to crap his pants, but I was too far gone in the moment to apologize.

"It went down like that?" Leon asked. He was bent over laughing and clapping his hands.

"Yea, how about I knew the girls were from Terror Town but I didn't know that they could get down like that!"

"It was like the GD's and Moe's!" Leon stated, egging me on.

"Yea man, and the Latin Kings! Wait, wait, wait!" I said turning myself around in a circle.

"This ninja chick named Ashley jumped in the fight and TKO'ed Sarah. She knocked her so hard that both of us fell to the ground like..." I rolled my eyes in the back of my head and collapsed my body as if I had been knocked senseless. Leon let out another loud scream and stomped his feet, causing the table to shake.

"Ohh my God, Ohh my God!" Leon said gasping for air.

"Man, Lee. I swear you missed it."

"Well, while women were fighting over you, I was busy in here slaving." Leon said taking off his hairnet.

"Yea, O.K.," I said. "You probably ain't did nothing but

eat all of the dang on food up in this mug. Is that why I can't get no spaghetti up in this motha. Yo hungry butt. We tired of these sandwiches, and y'all too cheap to get some Miracle Whip."

Leon laughed out loud.

"We don't want no mayonnaise!" we both said at the same time.

"So, man," Leon asked. "What's up with you and Kandi anyway?"

"Nothing man, just friends. You know that."

"Yea, I know but…" Leon's eyes gazed off in the distance.

"Here come the GD's right now."

I smiled at the thought of seeing Kandi again. I turned away from the table and threw my hands up so that she could see us. She looked so pretty to me, even in the beat up old sweats that she wore to dance practice. Kim followed behind her and noticed us first. Kim tapped Kandi on the shoulder and they both waded through the crowded cafeteria toward us.

"Float like a butterfly, sting like a bee," Leon said as Kim threw her leg up over the bench to take a seat at the table.

"Ha, whatever. I was just minding my business, on my way to my study session when I saw Kandi trying to mollywop somebody. I can't even tell you what happened next."

"I can!" I said laughing.

Kandi's face began to turn red. The fight embarrassed her. I knew her well enough to know that she didn't want to be seen as that girl that fights over dudes.

"It's cool Kandi," I said reaching across the table for her hand.

Kandi snatched her hand from under mine.

"I know!" she said with her face all screwed up.

Dang, almost, I thought.

"What up family!" Ashley said as she approached the table.

"Hey, Ashley girl!" Kandi said greeting her.

Everybody said their individual hellos, but Leon caught my attention. He got quiet. His jaws clenched and left an imprint of his muscles across his face.

"Leon, right?" Ashley said looking him up and down.

"Ashley, right? Leon rebutted, returning his version of her stank look. The table was quiet as we all waited for the joke, but there was none, just awkward silence.

"Yaw'll ate yet?" Ashley asked breaking eye contact with Leon.

"Naw we just got here," Kandi replied.

"Well what yaw'll usually get?" Ashley asked. She reached into her jacket pocket and pulled out a wad of crisp dollar bills.

"Twenty wings!" Kim shouted out without hesitation. Kandi smacked her lips and I slapped myself on the forehead.

"Thanks Ashley, but we're good," I said, still laughing at Kim's broke behind.

"Naw man, my treat," Ashley insisted.

"Forty Wings!!!" Leon yelled from across the table, smiling at Ashley. Ashely paused for a moment but smiled back.

"Forty it is!", she said before turning to head for the counter.

"We gone eat good tonight," Kim said stomping her foot against the old cafeteria floor. We all continued in laughter and waited for Ashley to return with the tray of wings.

"Dinner is served." Ashely placed the tray in the middle of the table.

"Thanks," we stated in unision as we all dug in, hot sauce and all.

"Hey, Lee," I said dipping the last hot wing in the ranch dressing. "What time is it?"

"Time for me to get back to work, before I get fired again. It's 11:15."

"Up, time to go," Kandi said jumping up from the table. "I got lab in the morning."

"Yea, I got practice at six," I said, co-signing.

Kim took one last gulp of her pop. "Me too, I need my rest for that boring business law lecture. I can't afford to take any more naps in that class."

We all giggled because we could relate.

"Mitch, let me holler at you real quick!" Leon said as everybody gathered their trash and pulled on their jackets. Leon looked up and saw his boss peer from behind the kitchen door, so he took a few steps in the other direction.

"What's up, man?" I asked following behind him.

"Ah, that's the ninja that you were talking about?" he said as he stared in the girls' direction. I watched Ashley as she belted over, laughing at one of Kandi's jokes.

"Yea, why?"

"Watch her man," Leon said.

"Huh?" I said looking at him.

"I don't know much about much, only a little about a little, but wealthy girls like that don't usually kick it with people like us. Something's wrong with her."

"What... Lee man, you trippin'."

"Watch her, Mitch man, just watch her," Leon said walking backwards into the kitchen.

I jogged through the cafe' to catch up with the girls. I knew that they wouldn't leave me, but I didn't want them waiting too long.

"What was that about?" Kandi asked as I caught up to her.

"Man stuff," I said in my James Earl Jones voice, putting my arm around her. Kandi turned her body so that my arm slid right off of her shoulders, and slapped right back against my side.

"Y'all need a ride?" Ashley said as we exited the building. I followed behind the girls and walked out of the front entrance onto the concrete stoop. The fall air was cool and icy enough to put some pep in the laziest man's step, but many of the night-owl students seemed to be immune. They huddled around each other, trying to get their last nicotine hit before calling it a night. It kind of reminded me of the bums that used to huddle around the garbage can fires back when I was younger. The light from the fire used to stream into my bedroom like a night light. I used to peek out of the window and watch them pace back and forth, fighting to keep warm. I had come a long way since then; but at the same time, I wasn't too far away to go back.

"Naw, we'll ride with Mitch," Kim replied.

I noticed Kandi shoot her an ill look.

"OK, see y'all tomorrow," Ashley said, before bouncing down the concrete steps and landing on the sidewalk.

"I parked over here," I said, leading the way to the parking lot. I shoved my cold hands into my pockets as we maneuvered in between the white lines of the parked cars, until we found our way to my dad's old Beemer. It was a piece of crap to him, but it was a beauty to me. I shined that boy up weekly and took care of it like it was a brand new car. I smiled to myself as I approached my ride and saw how the moonlight bounced off of the blue paint.

Kandi and Kim piled into the car and we headed toward the dorms. As usual, Kim changed my radio station before we even turned out of the lot. She had a bad habit of doing that. I would have blasted any other girl, but I always let them slide. They were my buddies, scratch that, my *best* buddies. They got away with eating in my ride and I even forgave Kandi for that flaming hot and nacho cheese incident the other day.

We pulled in front of Lincoln Hall Dormitory and the girls hopped out.

"Bye, Mitch," Kim said as she opened the passenger-side door. "See you tomorrow."

"Bye," I said.

Kandi got out of the back seat and didn't say a word. I watched her as she walked up the stairs, without turning back in my direction.

"Kandi!" I yelled, as I franticly reached over, rolling down the passenger-side window. I was trying to catch her attention before she disappeared into the building. I must have said it loud because all of the college-age bystanders jumped and turned as if their names were Kandi as well.

"I'm sorry," I said as she gazed into the car from the stoop. She stood there for a moment, silently, as our audience waited for her to respond. Even Kim was waiting to hear what she had to say.

"It's cool," she said, smiling.

She waved *goodbye* as she turned to enter through the door. I watched as both of them made their way to the elevator and disappeared from my sight.

That girl drives me crazy, I said chuckling to myself, glad that I hadn't lost a friend. Satisfied, I pulled the car around and headed to my off-campus apartment. It was only 5 minutes away, but on a night like this, the drive seemed to take forever. The streets were empty and the darkness reminded me of an old "Jason" movie. I pulled into the complex parking lot and luckily I found a spot right in front of the building. I reached into the back seat and pushed all of my tapes under the passenger's-side seat. Just because I was away at school, didn't mean that I couldn't walk outside to find my windows busted out. I took one last glance into my rear view mirror. I didn't see anyone walking or hiding in the cut so I turned the key and relaxed the engine.

I looked into the back seat to make sure the rear doors were locked and took one last peek at the passanger's side door. Satisfied, I quickly exited out of the vehicle and closed the diver's-side door shut. As a precaution, I yanked at the handle. The door didn't budge.

I turned and headed for the porch, hopping two steps at a time. As usual, the door to the building was unlocked, but I used my key to get past the small, cold foyer. I climbed another flight of stairs to the second floor. I reached the landing and headed down the hall to my two bedroom apartment.

I opened the door and took a deep breath, glad that the hectic day was coming to a close. To my surprise, my few seconds of serenity were rudely interrupted. I violently coughed. I could taste whatever I smelled. I tightly clenched my lips and put my hand over my mouth. Using my foot, I kicked the door closed.

Man, homie what this that smell?! I said to my half-naked roommate sitting unfazed on my grandmother's old couch.

"What up man!" he said, way to happy to see me. "We have a chef tonight. Lindsey, stopped by to make us some tacos."

I looked over to the kitchen and saw a long-haired girl standing over a burning pot. Smoke poured from the pot as the girl frantically tried to fan it away with my oven mitt. Her efforts failed as the siren from the smoke detector began to disturb the moment.

"YOU WANT SOME?" my roommate screamed over the loud beeping noise. I didn't answer. I just watched as the girl scrambled, trying to figure out how to silence the detector and put out the small fire at the same time.

"MAN, JUST KEEP YOUR CHICKS OUT OF MY ROOM!" I said screaming back over the siren.

"WHAT?" My roommate yelled back at me, holding his ear as a signal for me to speak up.

"KEEP YOUR HOOCHIES OUT OF MY ROOM, HOMIE!" I said louder, just as the stupid girl finally figured out how to cut off the alarm.

"Ohh!" my roommate said, recognizing his epiphany. He was the only person that was dumb enough to let girls wander around our apartment. I was certain that he let Sarah's scandalous behind in my room. That chick was always plotting.

The Boojee Informants

"Yea... ohh," I replied back showing my annoyance.

"You want some tacos, Mitch?" the girl said interrupting us, as she put her hands on her hips, trying to look cute.

"No, you two enjoy," I said sarcastically, as I made my way to my room and slammed the door behind me.

I hung my jacket up behind the door and took a seat on my twin-size bed. I took my shoes off and examined them for dirt and marks. I knew Sarah and her yuck mouth scratched my shoes up during her little scene earlier today. After running over them with a tooth brush and some water, I placed my shoes back in their assigned spot. Right in between my new J's and my b-ball shoes. Cleanliness was next to godliness where I came from. I glanced at the clock and noticed that it was already 11:45 p.m.

A man's job is never done, I said to myself, as I took a seat at my desk. I searched the shelf for my Political Science book, sat it down and turned the pages to chapter seven.

I'll get to bed at two, I thought. *It's all good.*

TWO

Ashley

ERRRRRRT!!!! The tires screeched as I rounded the dirt road. Dust spewed from under the tires and dusted the windshield. I hit the brights and the light illuminated the animal that I was chasing.

ERRRRRRT!!!!!!!! I rammed on the gas and the sports car jerked forward from underneath me. The raccoon ran across the abandoned field searching for a place to hide, but there was no where for it to go.

"Wooooooooowwwwww!!!!!," I screamed as I gained on my prey. I could feel the blood rushing through my body. My adrenaline was pumping. I felt alive.

"Here we go!" I yelled, as the animal disappeared from in front of the car. I bounced in my seat as the car ran over the innocent animal.

"Haaaahahahahah!!!!" I laughed as I slowed the car. I could hear the engine subside as the dials on the dashboard relaxed. I turned the high-powered vehicle around and came back to the spot of the unfortunate scene. I had to see the damage that I had caused. It was the only way to end my night. I turned the key and the engine cut off, but the strong battery kicked in. It was a dark night in the corn fields of the college town and I needed the light to see. I reached for the handle and pushed the long car door open. With my eyes fixated on the dead animal, I walked to take a seat on the hood of the car. The headlights gleamed on the carcass. It was so beautiful... the lines, the colors and the texture.

I reached in my jacket pocket and grabbed the square that I saved from the night before.

I wonder what Kandi is doing, I thought to myself. I struck the lighter, threw my head back, and inhaled the nicotine. A noise from the car caught my attention and ripped me from my trance. I blew the smoke out through my nose and slid off of the hood.

"Hello," I said answering the car phone.

"Where you at?" the man asked.

"Ohh, so you want to see me now. You were acting all funny earlier."

"Naw, man, it ain't nothing," the man replied. "Will I see you tonight?" he asked.

"Yea... I'm on my way".

SPRING BREAK

SPRING BREAK

THREE

Kandi

Where the heck are they? I asked myself as I bent down to search under the bed. I grabbed the part of the comforter that hung over the edge of the bed and threw it on top of the mattress. All I could see was a pile of dust and a few stale fries from the week before. Frustrated, I got up from my knees and paced the floor. I knew that I hadn't packed them. I purposely put them aside so I wouldn't have to pack twice.

Here they are. I reached under the desk and grabbed my shower shoes. There was no way that I was going to shower without them. Over the years, I had seen some pretty disgusting stuff in the ladies bathroom and there was no way that I was going to put my bare feet on that floor. It had almost been four years and I still hovered over the toilet seat when it was time for a number one and I lined the seat with toilet paper when it was time for a number two.

As I pulled off my PJ's, I glanced at the clock. It was already a quarter after twelve. I threw on my robe, grabbed my towel, shower caddy, and pink shower cap and headed for the door. I searched the pockets of my robe for my room keys before letting the door close behind me. Kim wasn't back yet and I was going to be pissed if I messed around and locked myself out of the room. Satisfied, I let the door slam, but the sound of our ringing phone caught my attention.

Dang. I frantically dug into my pocket to retrieve my keys. Suddenly I stopped.

It's probably Ashley's worrisome behind, I thought to myself. *This is her sixth time calling me within three hours.* Exhausted from her stalking, I rolled my eyes in the back of my head, shoved my keys back into my pocket, and headed for the showers.

As I walked the floor, I notice that it was pleasantly quiet. No yelling, loud music, or slamming doors. Most of the students had already headed home to take advantage of the spring break. I could have left yesterday, but there was no way that I was getting on the bus so I stayed behind to ride back to the Chi with my crew. I entered into the bathroom and headed for the corner shower, the one with the best water pressure. It felt good to know that I could shower as long as I wanted without feeling guilty. On any given day you could look under the shower curtain and see sets of wiggling toes desperately waiting for you to rinse and get the heck out of the way. But not today. I closed my eyes as the water bounced off of my back and relaxed my muscles. I was in heaven.

I was interrupted by the sound of the bathroom door creaking open. I listened to see if I could figure out who it was.

"Kandi!" I heard someone shout.

What the..., I mumbled to myself, stomping my foot in a puddle of water.

"What!" I yelled back, mad that my moment alone was ruined.

"Ashley's on the phone!" Kim yelled back, returning the attitude that I had given her.

"Again?" I asked.

"Yes, again!" Kim yelled from the door.

"Tell her I'll call her back!"

I heard the door close as Kim received my orders.

Somebody better be dead, I said to myself as I twisted the knob, turning off the water. I grabbed my towel and dried off. There was no way that I was going to rush out into the hall with water still on my body. I hated feeling the burst of cold air against my wet skin. I put my robe on, brushed my teeth and headed back to the room.

"What crawled up your butt and died?" Kim asked, as I entered into the room.

"Nothing man. I'm just tired of Ashley's stalking self. She called like six, well, seven times today!"

"I wanna be, I wanna be like Kandi", Kim sang, rewriting the Michael Jordan commercial. "If that girl could clone you, she would," Kim continued, using her finger to stress every word as if she were picking them out of thin air.

"I know!" I shouted, glad that somebody understood. "All of a sudden she walks like me, talks like me, dresses like me. Man, she annoying than a motha."

"She just looks up to you, girl, calm down," Kim said as if I was over-reacting.

"Calm down! How can I calm down when I can't even think straight. The dogon phone keeps ringing!" I balled my fist, tensed my neck and threw my head back in an effort to emphasize my frustration. Feeling as though I made my point, I melted back into my chair.

"Well, what are you going to tell her?" Kim asked, still laughing at my dramatics.

"I don't know," I said, pausing. "What am I supposed to say?"

"I need my own space"

"It's not you, it's me..."

"How in the heck is that going to sound?"

I stomped around the room and found my lotion. Deep down, I really didn't want to confront Ashley. I had no real tangible reason to be mad, except the fact that she annoyed the crap out of me. Maybe Kim was right. Hopefully, it will pass.

"Did you ever find out what her Dad does and how he got all of that dang on money?" Kim asked.

"Nope." I said applying the lotion to my ashy legs.

"Uhmmp." Kim replied. "Well if you find out, can you get me a recommendation letter?"

I stopped spreading the lotion and stared at Kim, "Do you care at all about this conversation?"

"Nope," Kim said smiling. "Only about getting into law school."

"You suck as a friend," I said. I reached for my dirty socks and threw them in her direction.

"Stank heifer!" Kim yelled dodging my laundry.

I glanced over at the clock that hung above my desk. "On snap! It's already one," I whined.

"Yeah, you better hurry up," Kim said, standing fully-dressed. She was throwing her last few items into her suitcase. "Mitch will be downstairs in 30 minutes".

I threw on the clothes that I had laid out on the bed and headed for the mirror. 'Yikes!' I almost scared myself when I saw my reflection. My hair was a mess. I put some grease on the edges, brushed it back, and put my long locks into a pony tail. I raced frantically around the room looking for anything that I had missed. We were only going home for a week, but I had to make sure that I had all of the necessities. Forgetting one handbag could be the difference between getting in the club for free or paying top dollar.

Ring, Ring, Ring! I just about tripped over my bag trying to get to the phone. I wanted Mitch to know that I was ready. If he knew that I was running late, I would never hear the end of it.

"I'm ready!" I said, with the phone halfway to my ear.

"Ummm, what…" I heard Ashley say from the other end of the phone. Annoyed, I used my hand, signaling Kim to put her bags down. I rested the phone on my shoulder.

"Hey girl" I said with a fake smile, my eyes rolling into the back of my head. *I could run but I couldn't hide.*

"Kandi, I really need to talk to you," Ashley said. I could hear her sadness through the phone.

"What's wrong girl, why you crying?"

Kim stopped admiring herself in the mirror and came closer to me. The concern on my face was reflected in hers.

"Umm…" Ashley's, voice cracked before she stopped to take a deep breath. I waited a moment, afraid to push her. She seemed so fragile, so broken.

"What's going on?" Kim asked, trying to whisper but unsuccessful at her attempt. Kim's prying scared Ashley. She pulled back.

"Never mind", Ashley said disappointed and still gasping for air. After a moment she caught her breath and tried to hide her vulnerability. "What time are you heading to the city?" she asked still failing to pull herself together.

"Now. Mitch should be downstairs any minute," I replied. Ashley remained silent. I could feel that she needed help.

"Ok," I said, wondering if I was about to make a mistake.

"I'll ride with you if you plan on leaving soon." I wanted to slap myself right after the words left my month, but Ashley was in need of a friend and I couldn't leave her like this.

"Just me and you?" Ashley asked, her spirits beginning to lift.

"Yea, Kim is riding with Mitch." Kim rolled her eyes and put her hand in my face before walking back over to the mirror.

"Thanks Kandi," Ashley said, sniffling. "I was just about to leave. Meet me in the lobby in ten."

I hung up the phone and began to gather my belongings. I was so confused as to what was all going on. I had never seen Ashley like that. She was usually so cool and nothing ever seemed to bother her. I almost felt like I was talking to a whole 'nother person. Somebody completely different. Something big had to have happened and I was almost afraid to find out what it could be.

"So I'll see you back at home?" Kim inquired, as I headed for the door.

I turned around and nodded my head. She was just as confused as I was but she knew what it meant to be a good friend.

"Be careful," she said, giving me a hug. Kim looked at me as if she wanted to say something else, as if more words were on the tip of her tongue, but she remained silent.

"Peace out. Oh, tell Mitch and Leon that I said 'Hi'." I threw my bags over my shoulder, walked backwards out of the door and let it close behind me.

I dragged my bags down the hall and hopped on the empty elevator. I watched as the numbers lit up. 3-2- 1, *ding*. I stepped out into the lobby and realized that the campus was even more deserted than I thought. I could see from the lobby windows that the parking lot was completely empty. No cars, no people, no nothing, all except for the shiny red Porsche that sat in front of the building.

"Hey," I said, as I opened the passenger door.

"Haaayy," Ashley replied, still depressed.

"So what's going on?"

Ashley took a deep breath and started the engine.

"Hold on, give me a minute," she said, as we pulled away from the curb. I stared at Ashley's eyes through her sunglasses. Her cheeks were puffy and her black eyeliner traced the flow of her tears. Her hair stood on the top of her head as if she had just stuck her finger in a socket. She was a mess.

We turned the corner and I saw Mitch's blue Beemer fly past us. He slowed as he turned to see if it was really me in Ashley's passenger seat.

Kim

I flew down the stairs when I heard the phone ring. I knew that it had to be Mitch and I didn't want to waste any more time. *Screw the elevator*, I thought as I jumped down the last three steps to the first floor landing. Mitch was standing at the front desk when I burst open the emergency door. He jumped at the sound of the door forcefully hitting the wall.

"We got to go!" I yelled running to the lobby door.

"Was that Kandi?!" Mitch asked jogging behind me.

If it was one thing that I liked about Mitch, it was that he knew when it was time to roll.

"Yea, something ain't right," I said as Leon opened the trunk for me to throw my bag in.

"I just saw them pull off! What's going on?" Mitch asked. He put the car in drive before Leon could close the door to the back seat.

"Just follow them. I'll explain on the way."

Kandi

We rode in silence for what seemed like forever. I watched Ashley as the tears continued to roll down her face. I thought that it would be a good idea to let her organize her thoughts, but I thought that she would be ready to talk by now.

Ashley reached up and used the back of her hand to wipe away another tear.

"Ash, man, what's wrong?" I asked, poking my head forward. I was concerned and trying to show her that I cared.

I felt the car speed up as Ashley bit her lip and silently stared forward toward the highway ahead of us.

"Ashley!" I said louder trying to break her out of her trance.

Ashley pounded her foot on the gas. The car took off like a bullet. My body violently jerked backward against the seat. I reached and hastily pulled the seatbelt across my body. Ashley ripped off her glasses and looked in my direction. Her right eye was blackened, and swollen.

"WHY DIDN'T YOU TELL ME !" Ashley screamed at me.

I was confused and scared out of my mind. I held on to the door and the seat. We were going too fast.

"What the heck are you talking about!" I yelled. "Slow down!"

"IS THAT WHY YOU DIDN'T ANSWER THE PHONE! YOU KNOW, DON'T YOU!" This time Ashley grabbed my face. She had the strength of a man. Pain ripped through my face as my teeth poked into the inside of my cheeks.

"ASHLEY STOP!" I yelled trying to pry her hands from my face. The speeding car swerved, I heard horns from the car behind us.

Ashley let my face go. She changed into a whole new person right in front of me. Her back straightened and her eyes widened.

"I'm pregnant," Ashley whispered over the roaring engine of the speeding car.

I sat silently, crying and praying for my life.

"I'm sorry Kandi," Ashley said, as she closed her eyes. I reached for the wheel to try to save us.

Mitch

Kim screamed as she saw Ashley's car swerve and just miss the street lamp. She threw her hands over her face afraid of what she might see next. I didn't know what to do. The car was going so fast. I had the pedal to the medal but there was no way that my old car could keep up with them.

I slammed my hand against the horn in an effort to get their attention but it didn't work.

"KANDI!!!!!!!" I screamed. Kim, Leon, and I watched in horror as the speeding Porsche flipped over and over and over again.

FOUR

Kandi

I was stuck in between reality and a dream. I could hear the mumblings and sounds swirling around me, but it was too hard to pull my mind from its permanent daydream. All I could see were bright lights dancing in front of me and flashes of my most precious memories playing across the cinema-like sky. I didn't belong here and I needed a way out of this zone. I fought and I fought to get out but the trance was too deep. It had control of me. The more I twisted and turned, the more the memories flashed like bolts of lightning. But there was a sound that was sent to save me. It was louder than all of the rest and the more I focused, the clearer it became. Like a dangling rope, I grabbed onto it and held on for dear life. I shut my eyes as the voice quickly pulled me up and through the clouds.

"Nurse, Nurse!!" My eyes began to focus and the voice became crystal clear. "She opened her eyes!" My mother yelled at the top of her lungs. She was leaning over me, her eyes welling with tears.

"She opened her eyes!" She screamed again. This time she was grabbing ahold of my hand. I felt the pressure of her touch and I used my little strength to squeeze back. I went to talk but I heard my father's whisper.

"Don't try to talk baby girl. Just relax." I followed my Father's orders as the nurses and doctor franticly stumbled into the all-white hospital room. All at once, I felt the pain from my injuries hit me like a ton of bricks. My head and my face were on fire and my chest felt like it had caved in. I moaned from the pain and tears began to stream down my face. The nurse quickly grabbed ahold of the bag that was suspended above my bed and refilled the contents. After a moment the paralyzing pain started to subside.

FIVE

Kandi

I had been locked up in the hospital for the past month and I was ready to bust out. They didn't have cable, radio, or anything. Well, they had cable but they didn't have the real cable channels that played the type of shows that I wanted to see. It was cool, though. I found other ways to entertain myself. I had a whole daily routine. In the morning, the nurse would come in and I would take the 20,000 pills to fight the infections, pain, whatever, whatever. Then I would flip to channel 5 and watch my daytime soap line up. After that, I tested out my spelling game with episodes of the "Wheel of Fortune".

But I must admit that the best part of the day was when the "Price is Right" came on. I would lay in my hospital bed with the cover kicked on the floor and my half-eaten lunch still on the rolling tray, screaming from the top of my lungs. "Thirty-five dollars and fifty-five cents you idiot!"

My parents would visit me every day after and before work and sometimes they would even spend the night with me, depending on which nurse was on duty. It was something about my mother that always made me feel comfortable. I turned into a big baby when she would check on my wounds, feed me my lunch, and rub my arms and legs when the medication made me sick. I was blessed, I mean really blessed. Through all of the wreckage I had lived, despite the broken nose, fractured skull, broken arm, and cracked ribs.

Every day wasn't a good day, though. Sometimes I would be in so much pain that I couldn't bear to get out of bed. I would just lay there, as still as I could with my eyes closed, hoping that soon the heavy dosage of medicine would kick in and whisk me back to sleep. Unfortunately, today was one of those days but I couldn't just lie and sleep.

From my hospital bed, I gazed across the room and out of the window. I sat straight up, with my legs dangling from the bed. Just like my mood, the sun had stopped shining and the sky had parted to let the rain pour down. My palms were sweating and I clenched my teeth when the sharp pains shot through my head. The clouds opened as a violent bolt of light sliced through them. The loud rumble of thunder followed seconds behind. The storm began to intensify right in step with my mental wounds.

The sound of the rain hitting the windowpane reminded me of the gravel pounding under the tires of the speeding car. I could see her eyes and the darkness that filled them. Maybe there was something that I could have said to save her. If only I knew what she wanted from me.

The thunder roared again, this time seeming to cause me more pain. I grabbed my stomach as I heard Ashley's voice, *"You knew! Why didn't you tell me?"*

I searched for the right answer but I didn't know what to say. I didn't know what she was talking about. Goose bumps began to form as I slid deeper into the horrible memory.

"Knock, Knock," Kim said as she, Mitch, and Leon waltzed through the door, dripping wet from the rain. They had no clue about what I was feeling on the inside. All they could see was the cast and the bruises.

"Hey," I said, my voice shaking. My eyes were still focused on the window. The rain had begun to slow and I watched the last drops slide all the way down the window and disappear. Just then, I felt the tear slide down my face and land on my jeans. Like the storm, my flashback was starting to fade.

Mitch walked around the bed to face me, blocking my view of

the window. He went to hand me the bouquet of balloons that he'd purchased, but his smile faded when he noticed the expression on my face.

"How are you feeling?" Concerned, Mitch bent down to get a good look at my face and carefully reached to wipe away my tears.

"I'm fine," I answered, somewhat embarrassed. The crew was used to me being the strong one. Now that had changed. I was vulnerable, hurt, and very fragile.

I tried my best to sniffle up the rest of my tears and I forced myself to smile. The room was silent for a moment as my crew fought to find a way to comfort me. I knew that they were there to help but unfortunately there was nothing that they could do. This was something that I would live with forever.

"No, really, I'm fine." I took a deep breath in an effort to calm myself and get Ashley's death out of my head. I tried to reassure Mitch by looking him directly into his eyes, ignoring the fact that mine were full of water. Kim walked over and had a seat next to me on the small bed. As she sat down I looked over and smiled at her. Her presence made me feel better. If anybody knew how I was feeling, it was her. We were two of a kind. She knew all of my secrets and I knew hers. Sometimes she knew what I was thinking before I even knew it. Kim didn't say a word, she just leaned in and gave me a hug. I hugged her back. I cried in Kim's arms for what seemed like forever. There were no words, just tears. Mitch rubbed my back while I continued to weep, releasing the fear and pain that I had been hiding for the last few weeks. I even saw Leon wipe away a few of his own tears. The crew was very patient with me. They all understood and let me have my moment. After a while, I was all cried out and the tears had dried.

"Come on, you ready?" Kim pulled away and looked at me. "It's time to get you out of here."

Sniffling, I smiled, raised my good hand and dragged my sweater across my face. Leon grabbed ahold of me, careful not to touch my cast, and led me to the wheel chair that Mitch had retrieved. I carefully took a seat and pointed to my bag over in the corner. Leon reached for it and took one more glance around the room for any belongings that I had missed.

"Say goodbye to this room," Kim said with her nose all turned up.

I chuckled at Kim's humor. Laughter was just what the doctor ordered and I couldn't wait to get a big dose of it. My hospital stay was over and it was time for me to resume my life. Mitch cautiously backed the wheelchair out of the room, careful not to bang my legs against the doorframe. We cleared the doorway and headed down the hall to the elevator.

It was kind of nice to have Mitch push me down the hall. I laid back in the chair and exhaled. Mitch made me feel safe. I knew that he cared for me and I loved it when he showed me. I looked at the balloons that he had tied to my luggage. *Hearts*, I thought. *I wonder what that means?*

Kim and I waited in the lobby until Mitch and Leon pulled the car around. Just like old times, we all packed into the car and headed home. I couldn't wait until we pulled up in front of my parent's house. I knew that my mother had planned a nice dinner for me and the crew. I could just see a whole table full of chicken, candied yams, mac and cheese, greens and corn bread. There wasn't anything that I wanted more than some good old soul food, especially after chugging down that stale old hospital food. As far as I was concerned, I didn't care if I ever saw Jello again.

Mitch hit the gas as we headed toward the expressway. Even though it was cold outside, I rolled down the window and let the cold air rush through. I was alive.

Mitch

I smiled to myself as a glanced over at Kandi. I watched as she lay back in the passenger seat. Her face was still sprinkled with scars. She looked over at herself in the sideview mirror, trying to catch her reflection. I knew that she was self-conscious about her appearance, but she was still the same beautiful girl to me. Soon the wounds will heal and her bluish green bruises would return to the color of her almond brown skin. Within a few weeks, her arm would heal and the cast that kept her arm propped against her chest would be sawed apart. The only thing that wouldn't heal was the memory. The memory of friendship, betrayal, death, and blame. I wanted to help that wound heal and hopefully my plan would do just that.

I turned on the radio and we headed toward the highway. Of course, Kim leaned in and wedged herself in between the front seats. She reached for the radio and flipped through the stations.

"Haaaay now!" Kim said as Mary J. Blige's "Real Love" flowed through the speakers. I pumped the gas pedal as I effortlessly merged into the Route 88 traffic. Just like old times, Kandi poked her lips out and bopped her head to the music. I swear that she thought she was in a music video. All she needed was some sun glasses and some background dancers.

After a few miles, I slowed the car and pulled over to the shoulder. I could feel the car shake as the other speeding vehicles whipped past us.

"What's wrong?" Kandi asked. "Please don't tell me that yo butt didn't get no gas."

I chuckled, "Naw man we got plenty of gas."

Leon and Kim sat quietly in the back seat. They were aware of what I had planned. Kim was all for it but Leon was strongly against it. I'm not sure why but on the other hand I just didn't care. Kandi needed this.

I reached and turned down the radio.

"Soooooooo, why did we stop..." Kandi asked.

Her voice began to trail off as she looked around and recognized our location. Her body became tense and her eyes began to dance in her head as she searched for a place to hide.

"Man, lets go!" Leon yelled from the back seat. Kim punched him in the side in an effort to shut him up. I ignored his comment and continued to talk to Kandi.

"I thought that you would want to say good bye," I said, reaching for her hand.

Kandi still remained silent. I could tell that she was fighting to hold back tears.

"Yea, Kandi." Kim chimed in.

"Her parents wouldn't allow any of us to go to the funeral and the way that they acted was ridiculous."

Kim sucked her teeth as she remembered Ashley's father screaming down the hospital hall that the accident was Kandi's fault. She vividly recalled when he cursed and spit at Kandi's name. Kim continued, "maybe you'll feel better if you say goodbye in your own way."

"But the chick tried to snuff Kandi!" Leon yelled.

"Shut up man!" I angrily recanted, jumping toward the edge of my seat. I had never been so pissed with Leon but this fool was out of line. I was ready to jump out of the car and dog-walk him myself. Friend or no friend.

Kandi looked up from her trance. Her eyes were welling with tears but I could see her strength.

"Yea, you right". Her voice was trembling. Ashley was haunting her and it was time for Kandi to put her to rest.

Kim, who was too annoyed to continue to sit next to Leon's bitter butt, flung the rear door open and quickly stepped onto the gravel. She was careful not to slide backwards down the steep embankment. But once she got her footing, she was sure to roll her eyes at Leon. She waited just long enough to slam the door in Leon's face as he tried to scoot along the leather seat to exit out of her side. Usually I would take that opportunity to remind her to not slam my dogon car doors, but I was distracted by my own efforts to safely exit the driver's seat. I stared in the rear mirror and waited for an opening between the oncoming traffic. I watched the speeding cars approach and fly past the window, shaking the blue Beemer as they cut through the wind. Off in the distance, I noticed one of the highway drivers quickly jerk his jeep and pull over to the side of the road. Drivers angrily honked their horns as it interrupted the flow of the other drivers. The black Jeep wasn't wobbling like most cars with flat tires, nor was smoke pumping out from under the hood.

When nature calls, I thought.

I pushed the door open and quickly made my way to the trunk. Leon followed, but his conscience forced him to walk over and help Kim get Kandi out of the passenger seat.

I popped the trunk open and retrieved the white wooden cross that I had assembled the night before. Together, we all cautiously headed down the dirty embankment, the same embankment that caused the red Porsche to go airborne before plummeting to the ground. I watched my step as we waded through the weeds and dirt. Kandi stopped when we reached the bottom. Kim gently pulled on her arm but Kandi refused to move any further.

"This is it," she said putting her hand out in front of her. She didn't want anyone to touch her. She just wanted to be in her moment. I walked over, careful not to disturb Kandi. She stood quiet with her eyes closed as I forced the cross into the frozen ground. No more tears ran down Kandi's face as she stood in prayer. She opened her eyes and ran her fingers against the top of the cross.

"Peace," she said under her breath.

Kandi turned and tried to head back up the embankment, but stopped when a flash of light blinded her. She threw her hand up as the sun reflected off of the piece of metal and into her eyes. She searched the ground to find the object that had begged for her attention.

"Is this my key chain?"

Kandi carefully bent down. Kim rushed over to help Kandi as she almost lost her balance. Kandi scooped up the key chain flipping it over and over to examine it.

"This is the key chain that my mother gave me," she said astonished.

"It must have gotten lost in the crash," Kim replied.

"Here go your glasses!" Leon shouted as he held the crooked, cracked frames in the air.

We all began to search the parameter for any of Kandi's items that had been left behind after the crash. Kim found a shoe, Kandi's school ID, and an empty wallet. I didn't find much, partially because I wasn't looking too hard. We had come back to the scene to help Kandi say goodbye, not to sift through crap on the side of the road. Besides, I had told Kandi's father that I would have her home sooner than later.

"Aye, y'all!" I yelled over the sound of the traffic up above. "Let's bounce! I got to get Kandi home."

"Hold on man!" Leon yelled back. "Come check this out!"

I took a deep breath and headed toward Leon. *I hope this clown ain't lookin' at no dead bird or no stupid mess like that*, I thought to myself.

As I approached Leon, I saw exactly what had caught his attention. Right next to the tree that had helped to claim Ashley's life sat a large book. It was made of leather and trimmed in thick layers of gold. The book glistened as the sunlight poured in from the parting clouds.

The Boojee Informants

Leon reached for the book to get a closer look. I ran my fingers across the old leather. My mind bounced around to the old black and white movies that came on cable T.V. and photographs that I once viewed in a museum.

This book has to be over one hundred years old, I thought.

The title was handwritten and was engraved in the leather with precision and care. The fancy cursive writing read *The Confidential Memo*.

Before I knew it the girls were standing by our sides.

"What is it?" Kandi asked.

Gently, Leon opened the yellow fragile pages and read the old hand-written note on the first page.

"This book is to be passed down our family tree as it will insure our status and wealth. There are only six other books of its kind and those have been circulated to the wealthiest families in the world. We should be so lucky that we were entrusted with the seventh edition."

In Confidence,
Bob Mathews

"Mathews," Kandi recited. "That's Ashley's book."

We heard Kandi, but ignored her at the same time. As we flipped through the pages there seemed to be a list of rules on how to run a business and how to maneuver in what is now modern day corporate America. It even had tips on how to make and keep money.

"Ay man, I think we hit a lick with this one," Leon said looking up from the book.

"Yea, man," I replied. I looked around, ready for the candid camera man to jump out from behind the brush. We had stumbled across information that most of the world would never see. The whole plan to corporate success was laid out right in front of us, the secret that was hidden from America's middle class and poor was right in our hands.

The excitement quickly faded as reality set back in. We were now in danger, a lot of it.

"Let's get out of here," Kim said, feeling the same as me. Leon put the book under his shirt and we hurried back to the car. Once back up the embankment Leon and I rounded the trunk and headed toward the driver's side.

BEEEEEEEEEEEEEEEEEEEEEPPPPPP!

The black Jeep swerved toward the shoulder of the road. Leon and I jumped back trying to hop on the hood of my blue Beemer. My heart was pounding, as the wind from the vehicle slammed against my face.

"Are you CRAZY!" Leon yelled after the jeep. I just stood silently as I watched the jeep speed off down the highway.

20 YEARS LATER

SIX

Kandi

It was Monday. Another bogus, wack, Monday, and as usual, I had to deal with some bull. Usually I would wait until Friday to let somebody go, but this little girl was so out of line that it had to be done today, messing up my freakin Monday. Her manager sent me some of her work over the weekend. I took one look at the docs and I almost fell backwards out of my chair. It was something that my 3rd grade neighbor could have done better. I was stumbling to decode the misspelled words and improper grammar, but after glancing at the chart that didn't even add up to 100% I was too through. This wasn't Maury, ain't no way we were 123% sure about a dangon thing!

"Hi, Ms. Jones," Victoria said as she entered into my office.

"Hello, Victoria, have a seat." I pointed to the empty chairs that sat in front of my desk. Victoria carefully stepped around my bearskin rug and had a seat. I watched as she nervously pulled down her skirt as if I hadn't already noticed its length. She knew what was up, but was just hoping for the best.

I placed the dreadful report on top of my keyboard and leaned back in my chair, careful not to harm my leather pumps. After a moment of pause I looked up to face the toothy smile of the young associate. Victoria had been working for me for more than two years and she really was a smart girl, she just lacked the 'intangibles'.

The chick came in every day at 9:15 and was always the first one out of the door. She took all types of personal calls at her desk, refused to mingle with her co-workers, and, as I saw first-hand, didn't believe in proofreading. Her manager was one of my best people so I had to go with his recommendation. He tried to talk to the girl, set her up with a mentor and everything. Either she just wasn't ready or I didn't share with her what she really needed to know. Sadly, I was convinced that it was the latter.

"Victoria", I said. "I'm sure that you know what this meeting is about." I was trying to think of the best way to start the conversation, but this was something that was never easy.

"Yes, this is about my annual bonus right!" Victoria was cheesing from ear to ear.

"I'm really excited, I have been working really hard."

I choked on my own spit as the words left her glittered lips. I patted my chest trying to stop myself from coughing.

"Do you need some water, Ms. Jones?" Victoria asked standing from her seat.

I waved my hand for her to sit.

"No, no," I said in between my last few coughs. "I'm fine."

I finally gained my composure and made a mental note to talk to her manager about setting expectations.

"Ummm, this conversation is not about your bonus… It's about your current probation status," I said reluctantly.

Victoria's face instantly changed. Her expression reminded me of Leon. The way her nose crinkled took me back to a time 20 years before. I focused and continued.

"As you know, you have been on probation for the past few weeks and you have already received two warnings."

"Yes…"

"Well, your manager and I reviewed your latest doc."

I reached across my desk and handed Victoria the doc filled with red check marks and large dark lines that cut through the sentences that she'd tried her best to craft. Victoria franticly flipped through the pages. Her hands were trembling.

"I'm sorry to say, but this is your last warning. I am going to have to let you go."

Victoria looked up from the doc and stared at me. Silently, I stared back.

"You set me up…" Victoria mumbled with tears in her eyes.

"I'm sorry," I responded, not hearing exactly what she said. I wanted to hug Victoria and tell her that she would be O.K. That it was my fault that she didn't do well.

"YOU SET ME UP! " Victoria screamed slamming the docs to the ground. She stood from the chair so quickly that it toppled over backwards breaking my crystal vase. The sound of the glass brought me to my feet.

"VICTORIA!" I yelled, stumbling almost breaking my heel.

"I worked my butt off for this bank and you're going to fire me! I made every change! Every change!"

Victoria kicked the docs and the pages went flying across the room like pigeons chasing after crumbs.

"Victoria," I said taking a deep breath trying to remain calm. I hit the hidden security button under my desk. This was about to turn ugly and I refused to have this type of behavior in my establishment.

"Nobody set you up," I said sternly, going into mommy mode. "You did this all by yourself. Hell! Look at how you're acting."

The word hell was a slip up, but by this time, I was pissed. I was pointing my finger and my lips were balled up. I couldn't believe that this little chump had broken my vase.

"Yea well, screw you and this bank, I don't care!" Victoria screamed. "This was just a first draft and not the final product, you sneaky bastard."

"Get your belongings and get out!!!" I yelled, pointing at the door. I'd had enough and now my Monday was really jacked up. The guilt that I once felt rushed out of my veins. I didn't even have that vase insured!

"Is everything O.K., Ms. Jones," the security guard shouted from the doorway, interrupting Victoria's tantrum.

"Oh you called security on me Ms. Jones!" Victoria shouted, now glad that she had an audience.

"Get her out of here," I said, calmly trying to regain my composure.

The security guard stepped in front of Victoria and created a barrier between the two of us.

"Let's go Miss," the guard stated, guiding her towards the door.

"I'll be back Ms. Faaakke Jooones!" Victoria yelled.

I could see everyone poking their heads from around their cubicles as Victoria yelled and kicked the doorframe. The guard grabbed her arms and forcefully dragged her down the hall.

"No you won't, we'll send you your belongings!" I shouted back down the hall. The whole office was so quiet that you could hear a pin drop. Everyone was focused on the drama and staring in my direction awaiting the next explosion.

"Back to work!" I yelled before turning back into my office. I shut the door behind me.

Dang, I mumbled to myself, before slamming my body down into my dark-brown leather chair.

O.K., what the just happened? I asked myself, pushing my hair off of my face.

I replayed the images in my mind and turned from my desk toward the picture frame window. I stared out onto the bustling Chicago streets. Even suspended at 23 stories, the sounds of honking cabs and aggressive traffic cops could still be heard loud and clear. My eyes followed the outline of the beautiful lakefront dotted with bikers and joggers, and down towards the south side of the city where I spent my childhood.

As I continued to stare, memories began to flood into my mind. I forced myself to remember when I was Victoria's age; young, dumb, and naive. I wondered how I made it through. How I became Kandi Jones, the owner of Jones's Financial. It had taken me fifteen years to gain the respect, experience, and money, but I couldn't have done it without my crew or the Confidential Memo. Victoria could have had a chance, but I was so busy building my empire that I forgot to help her. I was too selfish to groom her.

I smiled as my eyes completed the trail from my window all the way down to the South Side to one of the Jones's Banks. I took a deep breath and turned away from the window. On my desk sat a recent picture of me and my crew, all huddled together on a sandy beach with crystal clear water tiding behind us. We were all smiles in the picture, but I guess a vacation in Aruba would put a smile on anybody's face.

Kim, Leon, and Mitch had all managed to become very successful in their respective careers. Kim is an attorney with her own firm in California. Leon is one of the top surgeons at a prestigious hospital in the Washington, DC area and Mitch was just elected mayor of the city. The only problem was that behind all of our toothy smiles was selfishness and it was time for it to stop.

"Excuse me, Ms. Jones." The voice of my assistant ripped me from my trance.

"Is everything O.K.?" she asked, glancing over at the pile of broken glass.

"Yea, it's fine, Rosa," I said as she made her way over to examine the pile.

"I'll call someone to get this up."

"Thank you, Rosa. Also, can you call Jonathan in here for a minute."

"Sure, I'll bring him in."

Rosa bent down and carefully collected the largest remains of my vase. She was silent, probably too scared to talk, but I knew she was laughing inside. I was waiting for her to crack one m-f'ing smirk. Fortunately, Rosa handled the situation like a pro and headed for the door. I straightened up my desk and sent a quick text to Mitch. I knew that he would be pissed at my decision but he'd get over it.

"Hey, Kandi, you wanted to see me?" Jonathan asked, peeping his head into my office. He tried his best to play if off. I could tell that he was nervous. He had his hands stuffed deep into his packets and I watched his eyes bounce around my office as he took inventory of my damaged property.

"Yes, have a seat," I said, perky, like nothing had ever happened.

Jonathan slowly walked across my rug and over to the visitor's seat, but before sitting down he grabbed hold of the arm rest and shook the chair.

"It's not broken," I said calmly.

"Oh, I was just..."

Jonathan's voice trailed off as I shot him a stare.

"Sooo, how's it going!" he said changing the subject.

"Good," I said smiling.

Jonathan shook his head in agreement, but despite my efforts he was still on edge. I couldn't blame him. Just a moment ago he'd watched his peer get the boot, and now he was being asked to sit in the same hot seat. I decided to continue.

"So, as you know, we had to let Victoria go today."

Jonathan rubbed his hands against his slacks and shook his head.

"Don't worry, I didn't call you in here for that," I said as I walked over to close my office door.

"But I really need to talk to you about something," I said, turning away from the door. "Something very serious."

Jonathan searched his mind for the reason of our conversation. I was just as nervous as he was. My palms were sweating and my voice began to crack. I took a deep breath, but instead of continuing, I paused. I wondered if what I was about to do would send me to my grave.

"Ms. Jones?" Jonathan questioned.

I continued.

"I've been hiding a secret and I think it's time that I tell somebody."

"If you don't feel comfortable, you don't..." Jonathan began.

I put my hand up to silence him. It was either now or never.

"I want to tell you how I got here, how I got this, how I found you..."

Jonathan narrowed his eyes and cocked his head. He looked down at the rug, then back at me. I sat back down at my desk and reached for my stereo. I turned the dial to talk-radio and pumped the volume.

"I have the power to set you up with one of the most powerful people in the city and I can tell you secrets that almost nobody in the world knows," I whispered, leaning forward in my chair.

Jonathan leaned toward me and squinted his eyes in an effort to hear me better.

"But this is very dangerous. You have to promise me, for your physical safety and mine, that you will not tell a single soul."

"Dangerous?" Jonathan asked, throwing his head back.

"Yes. I am giving you the choice now. You can get up and leave or you can sit here and listen."

"Are you serous?" Jonathan asked, doubting me.

"I am dead serious," I said sternly. I slammed my hand against the wooden desk causing my photo of The Crew to topple over. Jonathan jerked at the sudden noise. My change in attitude shocked, but intrigued him. We were both silent and I gave him time to think. I watched as he nervously rubbed his hands together, as if he were seated in front of Thanksgiving dinner. Finally, he rested his nose on his folded hands. After a moment, Jonathan lifted his head and made direct eye contact. His left eyebrow went up just enough to remind me of where he was from.

"I'm here, Kandi," he said, sighing, throwing his arms out.

As Jonathan watched, I stood up from my chair and headed over to the painting that hung on my wall. I pulled at the side of the frame and the painting peeled away, exposing a large safe. With my back to Jonathan, I carefully entered the security code and scanned my fingertips. The door of the safe popped open. I reached in and grabbed the suitcase that lay inside. It was heavy, but I managed to swoop it up. I wobbled over to my desk and plopped it down with a thud. I rested next to it, my legs dangling from the wooden frame. I entered the security code and the top popped open and revealed what the crew and I had been studying for years.

"This is the 7th edition of *The Confidential Memo*. The ticket to my success."

"Wait, what?" Jonathan said perplexed.

"Relax," I uttered. "Let me tell you a story."

SEVEN

Kandi

The day that the crew and I left the scene of my accident we made a promise that we would reveal the Memo, but it was imperative that we waited for the right time. It seemed liked forever, but as planned, we used the Memo and strategically placed ourselves in elite positions allowing us to be in control of our careers and have access to the proper resources. All we needed was a young professional to lead the charge while we orchestrated in the background. We said that our project would go live soon, but I guess I just had to be the one to pull the trigger.

I watched Jonathan very closely as I told my story. I took note of his body language and his eye contact. He seemed very engaged and a little skeptical, but on the other hand, who wouldn't.

Jonathan had been involved in a youth group on the Southside of the city, which I once participated in during my high school years. As one of our ways of giving back, Kim and I would make sure to attend the foundation's annual banquet and donate to its fundraisers.

We could tell that Jonathan was different, even at the age of 16. I guess you could say that that was the beginning of his initiation. We kept a close eye on him over the next few years and, upon his graduation, I placed an ad for a job opening in the youth group newsletter. Just like I planned, Jonathan came full force.

I watched Jonathan as I finished my story, but I caught a glimpse of my wristwatch. To my surprise it was already 11:40 a.m. "Shoot! We have to go. We have lunch with Mitch at noon... Do you like sushi?"

Jonathan was trying to behave professionally, but I could tell by his face that sushi wasn't his first choice.

"Umm, sure," Jonathan nodded.

"We have to hurry," I said.

"I hope you're ready to meet Mr. Jackson, the mayor of our wonderful city," I said sarcastically.

I quickly grabbed my purse and jacket while Jonathan nervously waited for me to gather my belongings. I could tell that he was still absorbing the existence of *The Confidential Memo*, not to mention that he would be meeting the mayor of Chicago.

I reached for my keys and headed for the door. Jonathan followed behind me, trying to keep up.

Once we reached the cool spring air, I hailed a taxi.

"LaSalle and Wacker please," I said to the cab driver. Before Jonathan could get his foot completely in the door, the driver sped off into traffic.

We reached the restaurant at 12:00 p.m. on the dot, which was great because I hated to be late.

"Hello, reservations for Jones," I said to the maitre d', after she greeted me with her rehearsed lines.

The maitre d' searched for my name on her list, "Sure, right this way, Ms. Jones."

We followed her down a short hall. The walls were littered with photos and autographs of celebrities that had happily dined at the restaurant sometime in the past.

"Mayor Jackson has already arrived and you will be dining in the Executive Suite," the young lady said.

The maitre d' swung the double doors open revealing a dining suite built for a king.

"Well, well, look what the cat dragged in!" Mitch yelled, looking up from his Blackberry.

Mitch stood up from the table and removed the restaurant's black cloth napkin.

"Mr. Mayor, how are you!" I squealed, reaching out my arms for a hug.

It had been awhile since I had last seen Mitch. With our careers, it had become hard to keep in touch with the crew. Mitch let go of me and stared at my well proportioned frame. "Looks like you must be busy at the bank. How many of those kick boxing classes have you missed?" he said, lifting my arm and examining my mid-section.

I snatched my arm from him and shot him a dirty look.

"Just when I think we're going to have a good day, you go and be you," I said, annoyed.

Just as Mitch began to shoot his second insult, Jonathan cleared his throat reminding us of his presence.

"Oh, Jonathan, I'm sorry," I said, motioning for him to take a step forward.

"Jonathan, this is Mayor Mitchell Jackson." I turned toward Mitch, "Mayor, this is Jonathan."

Mitch glared at me like he wanted to scold me.

"The young man we discussed," I mumbled out of the side of my mouth.

Mitch continued to stare at me. I cleared my throat in an effort to break the awkward silence. After another moment Mitch finally spoke up. He had gotten his point across. I know that I should have consulted with everyone, but it is what it is.

"It's a real pleasure to meet you," Mitch said, extending his hand.

"The pleasure's all mine," Jonathan said, connecting the handshake.

"Have a seat, son. I've heard a lot about you."

We all pulled out our chairs and had a seat at the dining table.

"So, Jonathan, how is it working with Kandi?" Mitch asked, breaking the ice.

"It's great sir. I've learned a lot from her," Jonathan said, smiling at me.

I laughed to myself, remembering Jonathan's dumbfounded expression after I explained *The Confidential Memo*.

"How did you learn that you wanted to be in financial services?" Mitch asked.

"Well, sir, I've been involved in the Southside Outreach program over on 103rd since I was in middle school. Every month the directors would schedule professionals to come and talk about what they did, and one day Kandi stopped by."

Mitch leaned forward in his chair, "Why should I be able to trust you?" he asked bluntly.

Jonathan got quiet and thought for a minute. He was digging deep to prove himself. His eyes glossed over as he went deeper into his thoughts, almost trance like.

"I remember in grammar school, the teacher would go around the class and ask *'What do you want to be when you grow up?'* All you heard was teacher, fireman, police officer, doctor, or lawyer. I mean, nothing is wrong with that, but in my neighborhood that was all we saw. So that was all we knew."

Jonathan continued, "While everybody else was giving their answers, I would really try to figure out what I wanted to be. The vision would form so clearly." Jonathan sat up in his seat and used his hands to help make his point.

"I would have dreams about it and everything. Every time I would see myself all grown up in a suit, sitting behind a desk. There were papers all over and I had like three or four computers all running at the same time. I could even see the color of my office walls. They were burnt orange. It's unbelievable how clear it was, and still is. But when the teacher got to me and it was my turn to answer, I would just shout out what the other kids said cause I couldn't verbalize what I had envisioned. I had never seen it in real life before!"

Jonathan continued with our full attention, "Then one month Ms. Jones came to speak about her career. She told us about the different types of loans that companies need, interest rates, the stock market, and everything else. She also prepared a slide show and I swear, the last slide was a picture of a burnt orange office with a man sitting at a desk surrounded by three computer screens."

Jonathan looked up and made eye contact with Mitch, "I'm supposed to be here, sir. You can trust me."

Just as Jonathan finished his story the waiter approached the table and began to explain the specials. Luckily, Mitch and I had dined at the restaurant a few times before, because I didn't hear a word of what the waiter was saying. I was still stuck on Jonathan. His speech was so passionate and sadly similar to many others.

"Miss..." The waiter said, looking at me strangely.

"I'm sorry," I replied, pulling myself out of my thoughts.

I gave the waiter my order and he moved on to jot down Mitch's request. I glanced over at Jonathan who looked like he was having a difficult time making a selection. I could tell because he kept flipping the menu over from front to back.

"You should try the teriyaki chicken, Jonathan," I said giving him a hint.

"Oh yes, that sounds good. I'll have that with white rice," Jonathan responded, looking up at the waiter.

Good save, I thought. *This kid learns fast.*

I reached in my briefcase, pulling out a black three-ring binder. "Jonathan, this is for you. This is our version of *The Confidential Memo*. We will give you different lessons, piece by piece, as you progress in your career."

Jonathan smiled and reached for the binder, but Mitch grabbed it and pulled it out of his reach.

"You do understand that this is top secret, son," Mitch informed him, without flinching.

"Yes, Sir, I know."

"You do understand that I am the mayor, son," Mitch said in the same stern tone.

"Yes, Sir. I do. I'll make you proud." Jonathan promised, letting his confidence shine through.

"Well, good then," Mitch smiled. "Welcome to the family."

I firmly nodded my head to concur.

Thank goodness this went well, I thought to myself.

EIGHT

Kandi

Things were going good. The rumor mill had finally died down and Victoria's tirade was no longer the topic of conversation. But man it wasn't easy. I had to work hard to recreate the friendly environment that I had worked so hard to establish in the first place. I had formed employee focus groups, bought lunch for team members, planned meet and greets, and I had Rosa schedule a few company 'happy hours'. It took a lot of time and money, but it seemed like things were beginning to return back to normal.

Jonathan, on the other hand, was a work in progress. I could tell that he was studying the memo, but he was struggling to find his own identity in corporate America. It was something that we all went through, but I was positive that he would find his way.

After everyone left for the day I plopped down at my desk. I had been running from meeting to meeting and I was exhausted. After a short pause I opened my calendar and took note of all the tasks that I had to complete. I sighed, but pulled it together rather quickly. *Ain't nothing to it, but to do it*, I said to myself. But first, I had to get into the zone.

I leaned back into my chair and pulled my bottom drawer open. I rummaged through my CDs. *Come on, come on*, I mumbled to myself. *Ha!*

I grabbed the Mary J. Blige CD and popped the classic *My Life* album into my stereo. The sound filled the office and I began to relax. With the music humming, I reached for my newspapers and flipped through the pages. Most noted trends in the economy and mentioned notable bankruptcies and acquisitions, but there was one article that caught my eye. There was a sad story about a CFO who committed fraud and lost all of the retirement savings plans for 70 percent of the town's population. *That's f'-ed up,* I thought. "That ain't nothing but greed", I said, after shaking my head. I took one more sip of my coffee and got busy.

I went through the audit reports with a fine-tooth comb. Whatever I didn't understand, I made a phone call or took down a note. In my own company, I made sure that I knew everything that was going on. I dotted every "i", and crossed every "t". To some of my employees this was just a job, but it was my baby and I was responsible for every transaction.

As usual, I got lost in my work and before I knew it the CD had stopped playing and night had arrived. I called it quits at about 7:30 p.m., but before I logged off the computer, I took one last glance at my emails. To my surprise, I hadn't received any urgent show-stoppers. Feeling lucky, I leaned over to power down my computer, but the flashing light on my phone caught my eye. 'Dang', I mumbled. I had forgotten that I forwarded my calls to voice mail. I took a look at my watch, but decided to just go ahead and see who needed my attention.

Most of the voicemails were from the usual suspects about matters that they could handle if they put their minds to it. However, there was one voicemail in particular that caught my attention. It was from Eric Mathews, one of the bank's top clients. Eric's company, Clad, started out with the bank in its early years and continued to do business with us even with our limited capabilities, and even though we were just a community bank. Eric even introduced a lot of his acquaintances to the bank, which significantly helped to grow our commercial business, as well as our deposits. I owed a lot of my success to Eric, and because of his high profile, all of his business matters went through me.

I grabbed my notepad and proceeded to jot down Eric's matter as I held the phone in between my shoulder and ear.

"Hello, Kandi. This is Eric from Clad Co. Um... there is something very important that I want to discuss. It's about my daughter, Ashley Mathews. It seems that you two attended the same college at one point. As you know my company and associates hold a sizable concentration of your deposits, so I hope that you will be willing to clear your busy schedule. Meet me Wednesday, at noon, in my office."

Then he hung up.

I played the message over and over again. How did I not know that Eric had a daughter? How did I not know that she attended my university? How did I not know that Eric was Ashley's father?! I figured there was only one thing that would cause this type of meeting, *The Confidential Memo*. I picked up the phone and immediately called Mitch.

NINE

Jonathan

"What a day," I said to myself. I patted down my pockets and found my bus pass. This was the second week in a row that I worked just about 60 hours at the bank. I was tired, burnt out, mad, and hungry. Lately my hour lunch break had been shot to hell and instead of lounging with my buddies, I was stuck at my desk. I knew that working in corporate America wouldn't be easy, but I didn't think that it would be legalized slavery. Over the last few weeks I had really tried to push myself, but somehow there was a disconnect. There was always something that I could have done better; change this, change that... Sometimes I wanted to cock back and knock one of those clowns clean out, but instead I just stepped away to cool off.

I stepped into the street to see if a bus was on the way. Like I thought, no bus in sight. It was almost 10:30 p.m., long past rush hour and the frequency of buses had slowed. I took a look at the bus bench, but I decided not to sit. Ain't no way I was paying for dry cleaning, I was broke as it was.

Ms. Jones started me out in the bank's official credit training program, along with all the other recent college graduates, even though I was considered to be her analyst. She said I had to learn the ranks, from the bottom up. This wasn't all bad because it gave me a chance to talk to people that I usually wouldn't talk to. At first it was a little awkward, but, people are just people. Me and this one dude got real cool and he put me on to game. He said that the best way to launch a career is to get an internship with a large, well-known company because they usually offer you the job at the end. If that wasn't possible, then you should apply for training programs a few months before graduation because these types of programs allowed companies to "home grow" their employees and gave them access to information and opportunities that they otherwise would never get.

The sound of my phone ringing interrupted my thoughts. My favorite song blasted from the speaker and Nas' hard core lyrics sang out louder and louder. *Man, I have got to change that ringer.*

I looked at the phone and saw Peanut's name highlighted across the screen.

"Big P, what up!"

"What's good, Mr. Banker!" Peanut replied. "Where you been? How's the new J.O.B?"

"Man, it's crazy," I vented. "This corporate thang ain't no joke. Behind all them expensive suits is straight G's with loaded pistols ready to bust."

Peanut let out a chuckle.

"I'm serious, Man," I went on, stressing the "us" in serious. "These people will throw you under the bus in a minute.

"Man please," Peanut responded. "Them people don't want none."

I snickered, "Naw man, you don't understand. The last thing that you want to do is curse somebody out. You have to make them question themselves by using compliments mixed with passive aggressive behavior."

I wanted to share my new found knowledge, so I rambled on and on. "This whole thing is a game of chess and every move you make will affect your chances of kinging your opponent, and everyone is your opponent. Ohhh… Ohh! And there is a code for everything. If someone asks you to do something, you can't just say 'no'. You have to say, 'I'll try my best,' or 'I'll let you know when I get to it.' And if you don't do it, even though it was a question and not an order, they will send an email copying your boss. Man, corporate ain't no joke."

The phone was silent.

"Hello... Hello... Peanut!"

"Oh yeah, I feel you," voiced Peanut. "Umm, I'm a hit you back."

"Whatever, man," I said, rolling my eyes pressing the End button.

Just then the bus arrived in a cloud of dark smoke. I filed into line and I hopped on, along with the other corporate zombies. The bus was just about empty so I found my way to the back where I could stretch out without any repercussions.

'I wonder how Victoria is doing?,' I thought as I sat back into the seat. It had been a few weeks since I had last talked to her. I think that she was a little salty that she got fired, but I would never judge her. I know it's hard out here working for the man, especially if you're out here with no guidance. I wondered why Kandi didn't share the memo with Victoria, I mean she could have used it more than me. I took a mental note to call Victoria in the morning. Finally relaxed, I put my leg on the seat next to me.

'Oh snap.' I dug in my pocket for my phone, "It's been real, Nas." I scrolled down menu to find a new ringtone, one that wouldn't 'offend' the office.

TEN

Kandi

"Pick up, pick up," I said, while pacing my cherry hardwood floor. I had been calling Mitch all night, from the time I heard Eric's voicemail. I called him from my desk, the office lobby, my car, and now my house, all to hear Mitch's voice repeat the same tired voicemail greeting. I didn't want to call Kim and Leon yet, and screw up their night, when they were both halfway across the country safe and sound. But what if they weren't? What if Eric knew where they lived and sent someone after them? At that moment I held my breath, searched for Kim's number in my contact list and hit Send.

Kim picked up on the first ring. "Hi, Kandi girl. You still up?"

I gasped for air and rambled at the same time, "Ohhhhhh man, Kim. I'm sooo glad you answered the phone."

Kim instantly changed her tone. "Girl, what's wrong with you? What happened!"

I sat on the small chaise in the corner of my bedroom and told her everything. Kim was silent while she listened, a little too silent for my comfort. I wanted her to tell me that everything would be okay, that I was just tripping.

Instead, we both feared the same. The thought of being blackballed, blackmailed, sabotaged and physically harmed was all on the horizon. We had worked so hard to get where we were in our careers. The Memo helped us navigate through the system; it taught us how to play the game and how to move up the ranks. But it didn't teach us character, hard work, and discipline--that had already been instilled in all of us. After so many years I never thought the day would come when we would actually have to face our past.

I opened my mouth to express my feelings, but I was interrupted by the doorbell. Kim and I were so on edge that we both gasped at the loud sound.

"Who is that?" Kim whispered through the phone.

"Girl, I don't know," I whispered back. I felt like a little kid that just watched a horror film. I took a deep breath and tried to pull myself together. *Relax, it's probably nobody*, I thought to myself.

Ding Dong, Ding Dong, Ding Dong!!!! the doorbell rang again and again.

"Kim, if I don't call you back in five minutes, call the police," I whispered, before abruptly hanging up.

I tightened my robe and scurried down the hall in my fluffy house shoes to the guest room. The lights were off and the room was pitch black, but from here I could look out to the front yard. There was no way that I was going to the door without a clue of who so desperately needed to see me in the middle of the night, especially since my name was at the top of somebody's hit list.

I crept towards the window and slowly moved the curtain, inch by inch, to try and get a peek of whoever was standing on the front porch. Nobody was there, but in front of my house was a delivery truck. Its lights were off, but the white exhaust streaming from the back of the truck let me know the engine was still running.

"Who makes deliveries this late?" I mumbled to myself.

"CLASH!" The sound of glass breaking caused me to throw my back against the wall. My instincts kicked in and I quickly ran out of the room into the hallway. I hid in the closet to the right, at the top of the stairs. I tried to be as light on my feet as I could, but I was sure the intruder heard my feet pounding against the hardwood floor.

In the closet, I stood quietly as I heard the footsteps. I held my breath and my heart pounded louder and louder as the intruder came closer. The footsteps stopped right in front of the closet. From under the door, I could see the moonlight splash in from the window against the man's boots. My body began to tremble. I was trapped.

He turned away from the door and frantically ran into my bedroom. Without any regard for my belongings the crazed man rifled through my beloved possessions. I heard loud booms and bangs as my full length mirror was thrown from the wall and crashed onto the floor. He pulled my clothes out of my drawers, slit open my mattress and even pulled up my floor boards. It was clear that he was looking for something. Something he desperately wanted. All I could do was wait him out.

Another shadow passed the closet door. It was another man. He moved toward the bedroom.

"FREEZE!!! DON'T MOVE!!!" the second man yelled. The sound of the intruder ripping through my belongings came to a screeching halt.

"PUT YOUR HANDS ABOVE YOUR HEAD!!!" the second man shouted.

I heard the sounds of a struggle before a loud thud. My heart was beating fast with fear. I cracked the closet door to see what was going on and if it was safe for me to make my get-away. The man in black forced the man on the floor onto his stomach and proceeded to cuff his hands together.

The man in black yelled from over his shoulder, "Mr. Mayor, it's clear!"

Mitch didn't waste one second, "Kandi, Kandi, where are you!"

"I'm in here!" I yelled. I pushed further at the closet door, careful not to startle them. Mitch followed my voice and flew up the stairs, taking them two at a time.

"Are you O.K.?" he asked, grabbing my face into his hands.

"Yeah. But what's going on?" I asked, now confused more than ever. Ignoring my question Mitch gave me a hug and led me to the place that used to resemble my bedroom.

"Look at me!" Mitch yelled to the man on the floor. "Who do you work for?" Mitch yelled again, as the man in black kicked the man in his side with full force.

The man on the floor squealed, and balled up like a caterpillar. "I don't know her name!" he yelled. "I swear I don't know!"

"I'm a dirty, dirty, filthy, craaazzy cop," said the man in black. "If you tell me who you work for, I won't blow your head off. Now, WHO DO YOU WORK FOR!", The officer pulled his weapon from its holster and pointed it at the pitiful man lying on the floor.

"O.K, O.K.!" the man cried out. "I met a lady at a bar. She paid me to act like a delivery man to get some lady to answer the door. I'm supposed to be looking for some golden book."

"Is that right!" Mitch said with a blank stare. "SHHHHEEE paid you."

The man nervously nodded his head.

"He's lying! Get him out of here! We'll deal with him later," Mitch said with disgust.

The cop grabbed the man by his hair and forced him to stand. The man had a name tag on his collar that read the initials "A.V.M." A knee to the back forced him to move his feet. He moaned in pain as the cop dragged him away.

I was completely in shock. Someone had been sent to find the Memo with orders to take me out. So many thoughts ran through my head, but I couldn't speak.

"Kandi," Mitch said, interrupting my thoughts. "Pack what you can. We have to get out of here. It's not safe."

I threw on a tank top and a pair of jeans that were sprawled on the floor, and quickly began to grab whatever I could carry.

Mitch was talking while I hopped across the room to grab my valuables.

"One of my top campaign contributors called my office today. He threatened to pull all his funding if I don't show up for a meeting tomorrow."

What the heck is he talking about? I thought. *I almost died tonight and he's telling me about his day at the office.*

Mitch continued, "This man has helped me immensely during the last election and I didn't even realize who he was... Ashley Mathews' father..."

I stopped dead in my tracks, completely at a loss for words.

"Once I got the call, I ordered a tail to follow you to make sure you were safe. I also called in favors for officers to tail Kim and Leon."

I walked up to Mitch, finally able to process all the events of the day. "Eric called the bank today, too. He's one of my biggest clients, practically helped me open the bank. He alluded to withdrawing his funds if I don't show up for some meeting tomorrow, probably the same meeting."

Mitch's jaw hit the floor. "You mean this man has been in our lives all this time and has control over us! Man, we got played!" Mitch slammed his hand against the wall cracking the dry wall.

The phone rang loudly, causing both of us to jump.

"Kim. It's Kim," I mumbled.

ELEVEN

Kandi

    I lay my head against the window as the car quickly sped along the expressway. Mitch's bodyguard drove like a bat out of hell. His eyes were on the rearview mirror more than the road. We bobbed in and out of traffic, dodging the bright red brake lights of the night commuters. Annoyed, I looked down at my purse as it buzzed again for the third time since we left my house. Usually I would not have hesitated to rip through my purse to retrieve my Blackberry, but tonight was different. After what had just happened, work was the last thing on my mind. I just sat and watched as my purse vibrated along the floor.

    "Are you going to get that?" Mitch asked, sliding his phone away from his mouth.

    I reached down, grabbed my purse and dug deep to find the phone. There was nothing unusual, just a few missed emails from workaholic bankers. I continued to scroll down the screen in search of any showstoppers. None of those, but there was one email that caught my attention. It was from Jonathan:

Hello Kandi,

Attached below is the renewal for the $5MM line of credit for ETW & Co. Please review and let me know of any changes. Also, I will be out of the office tomorrow morning as I have a call with the owner of A.V. Manufacturing in Hillside (Victoria gave me the lead). The meeting is at noon and I expect to return to the office later in the afternoon. Please call my cell if you have any questions.

Thank You.

I chuckled to myself. My spirits rose as I read the email. 'Jonathan is a beast', I thought. He was already using the *Confidential Memo* against me: sending emails this late at night and using his network to meet with prospective customers. It annoyed me that he was still talking to Victoria, but there was nothing that I could do about that.

I wasn't concerned about Jonathan spending time away from the office, after all he had cleared it with me last week. While I was grabbing coffee in the break room, Jonathan had approached me with the song and dance routine. He said that client interaction would help him grow into his role at the bank and that he wanted to meet with prospects once a month. He had me cornered. What was I supposed to say as his boss, 'No, we don't do career growth in this office!' His request was more than reasonable and a 'no' could somehow come back to haunt me.

"Are you ready for the conference call?" Mitch asked, hanging up his call.

"Yeah, sure," I replied, somewhat nervously.

Mitch dialed Leon and conferenced in Kim, who were both on their way to their city's airports. Mitch had arranged for all of us to be in the same city by tomorrow morning. Once everyone was on the line, Mitch hit the speakerphone.

Mitch immediately asked, "Leon, Kim, do you have any dealings with this guy?"

"Yeah," Kim and Leon both answered solemnly.

Mitch threw his head back against the seat out of disgust.

Leon informed, "Eric sits on the board of the hospital where I work and apparently he is the brother of one of the principals at Kim's firm."

Kim chimed in, "It seems as though he was directly involved in your and Kandi's careers, and that could be simply because of location."

Makes sense to me, I thought. *That's why Mitch and I were the only ones summoned to the meeting.*

"So, what are we going to do?" Mitch asked, rubbing his hands against his thighs. "If he doesn't kill us then he could choose to ruin our careers. Pick your poison."

Leon spoke up, "What about the boy?"

"Jonathan's fine." I responded. "I know him, he didn't say anything."

"I hope you do," Leon responded.

"How do we beat this guy?" Kim jumped in, ignoring Leon and his attitude.

"There has to be something that we have that he doesn't, something that we could use to our advantage."

There was silence, as we all stopped to think for a moment.

"We have each other and connections of our own, not to mention old friends in old places," Kim added. "Eric and his goons had made it painfully clear that the only way we are going to make it out of this alive is as a team. Our way into this mess may be our way out."

"Yeah, Mitch, man," Leon said. "If you weren't there for Kandi, then who knows what would have happened. If you think about it we've already ruined one of his plans."

I turned away from the window, finally ready to share my epiphany, "We have to go to the meeting!"

"What?" Mitch exclaimed. He looked at me as if I had three heads. "Do you remember what just happened. Are you trying to get whacked?"

"Kandi, we really need to think about this," Kim interjected.

I spoke somewhat calmly, but with the attitude of a raging bull. "Memo or no Memo, I worked hard to get where I am today and no Eric Mathews is going to pull a little string and cause my whole world to unravel."

Leon took a deep breath. "You're right, Kandi…" Then he paused for another moment. "I'm game if you are."

"Me too!" Kim replied.

The airwaves were silent as I stared at Mitch, burning a hole through his forehead with my eyes.

"Okay, okay, calm down!" Mitch snapped, looking back in my direction. "Kandi, do you still have that connect at the news station?"

I raised my eyebrow, wondering what Mitch was thinking, "Yeeeaaa."

Mitch smiled back, sarcastically cutting his eyes at me.

"All right, I have an idea…"

TWELVE

Jonathan

    The weekend had finally come and I was ready to get it in. It had been a long week of back-breaking labor and my two little days of freedom were long overdue. Out of respect for the neighbors, I turned down the stereo system as I pulled in front of Peanut's house. Tonight was to be a night of stunting, and my beater was not going to get the results that I was looking for. My mom must have been in a good mood because I usually got a flat out NO if she thought the conversation was even leading to me being seated behind her woodgrain steering wheel. For whatever reason she happily tossed me the keys on the conditions that I filled up the tank and took the car for a spin through the car wash, although I did leave out the part about Peanut.

    My mom absolutely hated Peanut. Even though we grew up together she thought he was a bad influence…whatever that means. Nevertheless, I have my own mind and make my own decisions. She was crazy to think that I was dumb enough to let someone run me. So, by omitting Peanut's name, I avoided the argument. It was like taking candy from a baby. I agreed to her conditions, put my seat belt on as she watched from the window, and as soon as I was out of her sight I plowed down on the gas.

The Boojee Informants

As usual, Peanut wasn't ready when I arrived so I opted to sit in the car. After about ten minutes, Peanut finally emerged from the brick three-flat.

"Awwwwww weeeee!.," Peanut squealed, with his right fist up to his mouth. I sat nonchalantly leaning back in my mother's plush ride.

"Man, your mom let you use the ride tonight?" Peanut shouted, jogging up to the truck. He stopped in his tracks. "Wait...! Does this mean you have a curfew? Do you have to be back home by ten?" he said joking.

"Whatever, Man!" I yelled back, but giggling to myself as his statement was half-true. Peanut hopped in and clapped his feet together before closing the door.

Earlier that day I had gotten a text invite to one of the hottest clubs in the city and I couldn't wait to get there. Peanut and I always shut the club down. Nobody could resist our swag. Not to mention that Peanut was known in the streets. He always knew somebody that could land us in the V.I.P. and tonight, with my mother's ride; we were bound to have a record-breaking night.

I turned onto Stony Island and headed south to get onto the expressway. Peanut flipped through the tracks of our favorite mix CDs until he found a track that had enough base to cause a mini earthquake. I tried to gun the gas a few times, but traffic was heavier than usual for a Saturday night. I didn't pay it much attention until I had no choice but to slam on the brakes.

"What's going on!" I shouted in frustration. I absolutely hated traffic. I didn't understand how traffic jams even developed. If everybody knew how to drive and kept it moving, traffic jams would be a thing of the past. Well, at least in my mind.

"Maybe there was an accident," Peanut replied. "Turn onto 93rd, and bend left. I know a shortcut."

I followed Peanut's orders and veered left only to see that I was blocked in by red flares. I sat up to try and look pass the cars in front of me. I could see that flares forced the four lanes in front to merge into one. In a distant parking lot, there was a line of police cars and officers.

"Ummm, I think we just got stuck at a police check," I said, without flinching. Police checks were something of the norm on my side of town.

"Whaat!" Peanut yelled. He jumped up to get a better view out of the passenger window, but only caught a glimpse of the back of a pickup truck. Unsatisfied with the view, Peanut leaped over the armrest. His excitement startled me. I slammed down harder on the brakes and the truck jerked violently. Within seconds we were surrounded by blue and white lights.

A cop ran up to the driver's side window, "License and registration!" he ordered with his hand on his holster.

I showed my hands and slowly reached for the information in the glove compartment. Another cop approached the passenger side window and began to question Peanut. I handed my information to the cop, but as usual, it wasn't enough.

"Step out of the car!" the tall cop demanded.

I complied, slowly getting out, with my hands in plain view. Peanut did the same.

"Put your hands on the hood and spread your legs!" The officers ordered, this time shouting at us.

We both complied.

The cops proceeded to search both of us, rummaging through the car and my pockets. As expected, the cop found nothing on me except my house keys and a pack of chewing gum, but my heart dropped when the cop pulled a dime bag of weed from Peanut's back pocket. It just got real.

THIRTEEN

Jonathan

BEEP, BEEP, BEEP! My alarm clock rang loudly, jerking me awake from my nightmare. I opened my eyes and rolled over. It was already 5:30 in the morning and I could have sworn that I had just closed my eyes an hour ago. I lay in bed a moment longer to recall that devastating weekend home from college. I spent two nights in jail awaiting Monday morning bail. My parents' lecture during the ride home was more torturous than the mystery meat sandwich and the freezing, decrepit bunk bed in jail. Not only had I let my parents down, but I disrespected myself in the process. From that day on, I promised myself that I would never see the inside of a jail again, nor would I ever put myself in a position to be looked down upon by anyone.

Even though the charges were dropped, the record of the arrest caused me a lot of unnecessary grief. Before I had gotten the job at the bank I had been on six different interviews for some very prestigious companies. The interview processes were grueling, but I stayed consistent and kept my game face on. Each and every time I beat out the competition and got the job offer. But time after time again, the job offer was followed up by a rejection letter after the results of the background check were revealed.

It was such a depressing, dark time for me. I needed to keep my promise to myself and I couldn't do that sitting at home without a job. I was supposed to be out in the world making a difference and building a career that I could be proud of. Instead, I was on the couch watching time go by. Just as I was about to give up, Kandi Jones came along. She didn't let my one and only mistake ruin my chances to work for her bank. Even though Kandi was never arrested before, somehow she was able to relate to my situation and reserved judgment. She gave me a second chance and for that, I am grateful.

I jumped out of bed and continued on with my morning ritual. I logged onto the Web and checked the balance of my savings and checking accounts. Since I started earning my own living, I miraculously understood the value of a dollar. I cut back on mall visits to purchase high priced, name brand clothing, and I used the extra cash to build a nest egg. I wanted to position my money to make money, and that was exactly what I was doing.

Next, I reached in my briefcase and retrieved my calendar to check for today's scheduled meetings. Today I had a meeting with a business owner. Victoria's mother had started a manufacturing firm and she set us up to meet. I know that I'm just an analyst, but I placed myself in the fast-track program at the bank to be promoted, and as we all know, you have to do the job to get the job.

I thought about my co-workers reaction if they were to find out that I was scheduling my own calls. I'm sure they would be jealous because they didn't think of the idea, but that was the difference between me and them. I challenged myself and I didn't need anybody to tell me how and when to do something. I learned from my mistakes, listened to advice from the experienced, and constantly critiqued myself.

I made another mental note to pull in one of the best and most seasoned bankers to help close the deal, if it ever came to that. So far I didn't have any goals to meet, so I figured it would be best to gain a good friend in a high place. 'Another pawn off the chess board,' I thought.

I hit the radio button on my alarm clock and my favorite song blared from the speaker.

FOURTEEN

Kandi

I nervously waited in the old coffee shop for everyone to arrive. It was a quarter to 11 a.m., which meant the crew wasn't late, yet. Mitch and I had spent an uncomfortable night in the 'burbs at his safe house. It didn't matter how many of Mitch's big burly guards surrounded the property, there was no way that I was getting any sleep. After Mitch left in the morning to meet Leon and Kim at the airport, I got the O.K. to leave and get some air. I needed to clear my mind of what was to come later today. All it took was a short walk around the corner before I stumbled across the little coffee shop with a statue of a donut in the front window.

The small shop was crowded, but I found a seat at a small table for two in the back. Shortly after getting situated, I noticed a man dressed in all black enter the door. I had thought I freed myself from Mitch's dungeon, but I guess I was wrong. *Man, it's hard to shake these guards*, I thought. I made eye contact with the guard letting him know to back off and leave me to myself. He obliged, sitting in a far corner.

"May I help you?" a young girl asked. Her apron was soiled as if she had been baking the donuts herself.

"Yes, I'll just have coffee, two creams and two sugars, please."

The Boojee Informants

"Sure, no problem," the girl replied.

Within a few moments the girl returned with a pot of black coffee and poured it into an old white mug. "Let me know if you need anything else," she said, tossing the packets of cream and sugar on the table.

I sipped my coffee and looked around at the other patrons. Many looked overworked or just plain beat down by life. I'm sure a few of them had never dreamed that they would be humping daily on a job that they hated, or working their fingers to the bone with no power or appreciation on the job. But little did they know that there is a plan to make it to the top and I had it right in my bag. I thought about tossing the Memo on the floor into the middle of the restaurant and high tailing it out the door to a different city, using a different name. But I'm sure the crowd of over-caffeinated corporate zombies would just step right over the Memo and assume that I just forgot to pay the meter.

Just like clockwork, I heard a car horn blow three times. That was the signal. I left a $5 bill on the table, grabbed my bag, and headed for the door. The guard followed close behind.

Out front was Mitch's black limo and a news van sat behind it. *I guess the plan is on*, I thought to myself, as the driver opened the door for me.

"You got the stuff?" Mitch asked.

"Yeah, I got it," I replied.

"Good, then we shall proceed," Mitch stated.

I greeted Kim with a hug as the limo pulled away from the curb. The news van followed. On the way there, Kim tested Mitch's recording equipment and cross-checked it with Leon, who rode in the news van with four of Mitch's guards. She also helped me attach the microphone to my undergarments.

Through the help of an old friend at the news station, we had put together a sting to record Eric's conversation admitting the existence of *The Confidential Memo*. The public would learn all about the Memo on the 5 o'clock news. The plan was that this would cause a huge backlash against public figures, the rich, and whoever else was assumed to have laid eyes on the Memo. We knew that we would possibly be opening Pandora's box, but it was the only card that we had left to play.

Once we got closer to Eric's office, the news van began to blend in with traffic, trailing us at five car lengths. When we finally arrived,

Mitch's limo snailed up the circular driveway and parked in front of the elaborate entrance. The driver got out and walked around the long car. I nodded goodbye to Kim as the driver opened the door. I wasn't sure if this would be the last time I would see her, but I refused to speak it. Kim nodded back. She had the same train of thought as me. I grabbed the driver's hand and stepped out of the car onto the hard concrete. I straightened out my navy suit as Mitch took his place next to me. Without missing a beat, we both headed for our destiny or doom.

"Hello, Mindy. How are you today?" I inquired. As always, I was nice to Eric Mathews' long time assistant. I was trying hard to hide my uneasiness.

"Good morning, Kandi. It's nice to see you. Good morning, Mayor. How are you?" Mindy greeted.

"I'm fine, Mindy. Is Eric available?" It was just like Mitch to cut to the chase when he was nervous.

"Yes. He's expecting you," Mindy said. She moved from behind her desk and we followed her down the long corridor to the main boardroom. Mindy swung open the double doors to reveal the upscale room, decorated with dark wooden furniture and fine oil paintings. Eric was already seated at the head of the massive table. He was looking down at the newspaper. He didn't acknowledge our presence when we entered the room; he just kept his head down, looking at the paper. The tension was thick and not even the view of the peaceful grassy common area from the crystal clear window could keep the room from feeling ice cold.

Mindy interrupted the awkward silence. "Do you want some water or coffee?"

Mitch shook his head *"No,"* but I mustered up the courage to say, "No, thank you."

Mindy turned and left the room, closing the massive double doors behind her.

Mitch and I just stood for a moment before we decided to take a seat at the table, but first I managed to take a long look at Eric. The heavy bags under his eyes made it obvious that he had endured more than a few long nights. He hadn't shaved in days and his rumpled clothing hung off of the frame that was ten pounds lighter than my last memory of him. Eric reached up to brush his silky white hair out of his face and let out a loud sigh. He then violently pushed the newspaper into the middle of the table and ripped his glasses from his face.

Stunned, Mitch and I didn't say a word. We sat quietly.

After a moment Eric began to speak, his head hung low, as he continued to stare at the empty space on the table. "You know... sometimes you can work so hard for something, just to have someone take it right from under you."

Mitch and I looked at each other, still refusing to say a word.

Eric continued, "My family has spent many years building a brand, and now in the blink of an eye, our name is tarnished over some foolishness."

I looked over and caught a glimpse of Mitch adjusting his tie with the hidden camera.

"I know you all knew my daughter in college," Eric stated, with his head still hanging low.

"Yes, we knew her." Mitch spoke up. He was cool and in control. Nothing like me. The thoughts of Ashley crept back into my mind. I had spent years trying to find a way to bury the pain. Sometimes when I slept I could hear her screaming, 'YOU KNEW AND YOU DIDN'T TELL ME'. I could feel my body tremble as the thoughts rushed back. My throat got dry and my head began to hurt. I tried my best to fight back the tears. I looked up to face Mitch. With his eyes he told me to hold it together and I did.

"Eric, I am very sorry for your loss. Your daughter and I were friends…"

"Stop, just stop", Eric mumbled, holding up his hands.

I took a deep breath and swallowed hard.

"Excuse me?" I asked. I couldn't fight it any more, I was sick of being the blame.

"Eric it wasn't my fault," I said sternly. Mitch wanted to say something but he didn't, he let me have the floor.

"Your fault for what?" Eric asked, pushing away from the table. "The fact that Ashley dropped out of school, her drug habit, my fatherless grand-daughter. Which one was your fault Kandi? Tell me that much."

Mitch and I were silent. What was he talking about, drugs, and grandchildren. I had not a clue.

"No Eric, Ashley's death," I said humbly.

Eric's body jilted as the words left my mouth. He leaned into the table, grabbed the newspaper and forcefully tossed it in my direction. I caught the paper before it slapped me in the face and I slammed it back onto the table. My heart began to beat faster and faster, as my temper began to rear its ugly head.

"Just listen!" Eric yelled banging his hand against the table. "Ashley's not dead, she was never dead."

"Wait, wait, dude what are you talking about Eric!?" Mitch asked pushing back from the table. He was pissed. He banged his fist into his hand to emphasize every word. "I saw the accident. I was there when they pulled her from the car!"

I sat and tried to take it all in. *Ashley's not dead?*, I thought. All of this time, for 20 years I thought that she was dead.

Eric stood. His chair rolled from under him and banged against the wall. "It was all a lie, all of it was a lie!" He said with tears in his eyes. "And all it did was make it worse." Eric walked over towards the window. A lonely tear slid down his wrinkled cheek as he turned away. "Ashley was one of those kids that needed a lot of attention, and I ignored her," Eric admitted, gazing out the window. "I traveled for work, and after the divorce, I had to leave her home alone a lot. I was too stupid to notice that the change in her attitude, dress, walk, and talk, was her way of calling out for help." Eric counted his daughter's red flags on his fingertips. "I tried to help her, but it was too late. She found the attention somewhere else. She got pregnant at school and was afraid to tell me. I made her feel so alone, so alone that..." Eric's voice began to crack and he stopped to take a deep breath. It was hard for the words to leave his lips. He used the window as support and struggled to continue, "she tried to kill herself."

I tried to chime in, but he put his hand up.

"Our family is all about image you know," he said, shamefully laughing at his ignorance. "We'd rather people think that she was dead than alive and pregnant. It was all good until I figured out that she had lost that stupid book." Eric stepped away from the window and back towards the table. "I searched, and searched, and searched, and then it hit me. Eric paused and looked right at Mitch, "I saw you all at the crash site, and I'm glad that I missed."

The Boojee Informants

Mitch clenched his teeth as he remembered the jeep that tried to run him and Leon down. I shook my head in disgust and looked down at the table. I could no longer look at Eric. How he treated Ashley almost made me vomit. As I stared down, my eyes ran across the headline of the article that Eric shoved in my face. I focused my eyes and read the headline: 'Matthews' Corruption'. I read on until I found the missing piece of the puzzle, 'Ashley Matthews, CFO indicted on corruption charges'.

"I read about this in the newspaper a few days ago", I said interrupting the deadly silence. This is the company that lost all of those 401k's?!"

Eric turned back towards the window and began to speak again. The room was so silent that you could hear a pin drop. "I let you all keep the Memo as an experiment. I've been following all four of you since that day. Despite what I was told about your class of people, you all used the Memo very effectively. Of course you had a little help," Eric said smiling to himself.

Mitch decided to get the show on the road. "So, what exactly is this meeting about, Eric?"

"I need that book Mitch," Eric stated sternly. "It's the only way that I can help my daughter." Eric's smile faded, once he saw the nasty looks on our faces. A dark shadow quickly passed the window as Eric stepped away from it. Mitch's security team was posted and they were ready for anything.

"That's bull, Eric!" I shouted, my temper now breaking through its barrier. "You stand here, and give us this sob story about Ashley! I ain't giving you nothing. What do you think, I'm stupid?!"

Eric was surprised by my outburst and charged toward me. A red dot streamed from the direction of the window. "I helped you to become who you are and this is how you talk to me!" Eric shouted.

Mitch jumped from his seat to block Eric's path toward me, as well as stop the threat of gunfire. Mitch's large frame caused Eric to think twice. Eric froze in his tracks.

"Oh yeah, Eric!" Mitch shouted. "Now you want to ask! The other day you sent one of your goons to kill Kandi!"

Eric cut him off. "Man, what are you talking about! I would

never try to hurt Kandi!" Eric paused, "Vickie said that you all were a bunch of conniving, scandalous liars! But I didn't believe her!"

"Now I'm the liar?!" I screamed over Mitch's shoulder. I worked my butt off to get where I am! And, and, and…"

"WHO THE HELL IS VICKIE?!!!!," both Mitch and I shouted at the top of our lungs.

"Victoria, my grand daughter!" Eric yelled back.

My mind went into overload.

"Ashley is Victoria's mother?" I said slowly.

"Yes," Eric said putting his hands up, ready to surrender.

"A.V.M…" I mumbled. I had heard those initials from somewhere, but I couldn't put my finger on it.

Mitch still wasn't satisfied, "Well if you didn't try to kill Kandi, then who did?"

"Ashley and Victoria!" I shouted.

Surprised, both Eric and Mitch turned to face me.

"No, Victoria has nothing to do with this! I told her not to take the job, she doesn't have a clue," Eric said taking a step back.

I cut him off, "A.V.M., those were the initials on the man's clothing that broke into my house. He said that a woman sent him."

Eric's face went pale.

"Eric, where's Ashley?" Mitch sternly demanded.

Eric stopped to gather his thoughts; it was all too much for him.

"Now!" Mitch shouted.

"She's at A.V. Manufacturing. It's an old vacant factory. They're trying to start their own business." Eric spoke slowly, as he was still processing the fact that his little girl was on the path to becoming a deranged murderer.

"We have to find Jonathan!" I shouted. "He's with Ashley right now!"

FIFTEEN

Jonathan

I turned into the parking lot of A.V. Manufacturing with five minutes to spare. Usually, I liked to get to my appointments a little early, but today I got turned around during the commute. The plant was located all the way in the back of an old industrial park and the streets zigzagged around each other. Not even my GPS could save me from navigating through such a nightmare.

I put on my turning signal and turned right, maneuvering into the parking lot. To my surprise, the parking lot didn't resemble any that I had visited before. Weeds grew in between the cracks of the concrete and I noticed trash along the side of the building. There was only one other car in the lot, which was also strange. Usually companies are bustling with workers and trucks pulling in and out to load and unload inventory. *Maybe this is the parking lot for employees and loading is around the back*, I thought.

I pulled into the parking space marked "Visitor" and took a glance at the large lettering that hung above the entrance.

"5364," I repeated. *I'm at the right place.*

I reached for my phone and texted Victoria. She couldn't attend the meeting, but I thought that it would be nice if she could meet me here after she finished whatever she was doing. She didn't know this,

The Boojee Informants

but I had planned to take her out to lunch. It would be my way of saying thanks for the referral.

After one last look at the building, I brushed off my doubts and took a glance at myself in the rearview mirror. I had to make sure there were no traces of the donuts I had just devoured on the drive over.

My very first solo call, knock them dead! I gave my reflection the wink for good luck.

As I strolled up to the door, I brushed my hands over my suit jacket. I hated that I had to wear an undershirt, dress shirt, tie, and a jacket every single day, no matter the weather. *Girls have it much easier, at least they can wear skirts*, I thought. I approached the entrance and reached for the handle to open the door, but it pulled back stubbornly. *I guess it's locked.* I looked around and saw an intercom system to the left of the door. I pressed the white button and waited for a response.

"Hello, may I help you?" a woman's voice said.

"Yes, Jonathan from Jones's Bank. Ashley is expecting me at noon."

"Oh yes!" the voice responded. "I'll buzz you in."

BUUUUUUUUZZZZZZZZ!

At the sound of the buzzer I reached for the door. I heard footsteps running toward me. I turned, just in time to see a wild haired woman swing an old metal shovel toward my head. Then there was darkness.

SIXTEEN

Jonathan

CLAP, CLAP, CLAP!
I opened my eyes to see a pair of hands waving in front of my face. My head was banging with pain and my sight was blurry. I blinked a few times, trying to get a clearer view of the objects in front of me. The room was dim, dusty, and cold. Only a strip of light streaming from an old broken window illuminated the woman's face.

"Wake up, buddy," I heard the woman's voice say. "That's right, get on up."

I felt something hot drip across my forehead. I tried to reach up to wipe the liquid away before it rolled into my eyes, but my hands were tied together. I looked down, creating another path for the fluid and saw the blood from my wounded head stain my shirt. I jerked my legs to try to move, but my feet were also bound with duct tape. I lay helplessly on the dirty floor wondering what was next, and why.

"If you scream, nobody will hear you," she whispered into my ear. I could feel her hot breath steaming the side of my face.

"Why are you doing this?" I asked. My head hurt more and more with each movement. "I don't have any money. You can have the car."

"Money?" she said, laughing out loud. "I don't want your pennies. You don't have to tell me, cause I know Kandi ain't paying you jack! My baby told me that." She laughed, slapping her knee.

The Boojee Informants

"What do you want?" I asked, still squinting my eyes, trying to shield the intense pain.

"I want the book," the women said softly.

"What book?" I asked.

The women stood and walked away from me. She paced around the filthy factory floor, mumbling to herself. I could hear the sound of her heels hitting the concrete floor with her every step. Finally, she took a seat on an old milk crate in the corner of the room.

"Do you know who I am?" She asked, while examining her dirt-stained manicure in the dim light.

I was afraid to answer. I didn't know if it was a trick question.

She continued, "I'll take that as a NO. My name is Ashley MATHEWS."

I thought back to the story that Kandi told me about her college days. Was this the Ashley that Kandi and the Crew got the *Confidential Memo* from? Isn't she dead? My eyes grew wide as I started to realize exactly who had taken me hostage.

Ashley was reading my facial expression, "Yeah, that's me! The ghost of your boss's messed up past!" Ashley continued, "Look-ee here boy," she said smacking her lips. "I have been through some mess. I mean some reeeaal mess. A long time ago my father gave me something and told me that it was my key to success. At the time I wasn't trying to hear that clown. But due to recent events I think that he may have been onto something. Don't you think it will come in handy?" Ashley stood and twirled in a circle, trying to show off the dirty, run-down facility.

Ashley smiled at me and began to pace the dusty floor. "So I thought and thought about the last person that may have seen that book and you know who I thought of?" Ashley paused. "Kandi," she said.

I mean, how else could she become a bank owner? How else could Mitch become mayor? Because they have the *Confidential Memo*!"

Ashley threw her hands in the air as if she had just solved the world's problems. "And oh yea, why in the world would my father be stalking them? He thinks I'm crazy, but I got eyes and ears. I can figure it out."

Ashley stopped and scratched her head, "You're her little lab rat, right? At least that's how Victoria made it sound."

"Victoria, " I replied still dazed.

"Oh, yea, that's my kid," Ashley said smiling. "She still can't figure out why I forced her to get that job, but she messed it all up when she got fired. This could have been easy." Ashley paused and turned her attention back to me. "Now, boy, where's the memo?" she asked nicely.

"I don't know…" Ashley cut me off.

"My father lied to me just like you are doing!" She reached behind her back and pulled out a gun. She stood and pointed it in my direction. "Now where's the Memo!"

"I don't know!" I yelled.

BOOOM! Ashley pulled the trigger. The bullet hit a pipe above my head, and steam came rolling out.

"Kandi never gave me the Memo! She only gave me a summary! It's in my car!" I sang like a bird. I was now squirming to free myself of the duct tape.

Ashley moved toward me, bent down and looked deep into my eyes. After a moment, she uttered, "Umm... You may be the only man on earth that doesn't lie. What am I going to do with a summary?" Ashley moved along the side of me and grabbed at my arm.

"Get up!" She shouted.

She pulled my arm to help me up and held the gun to my back. I struggled to stand on my bound feet.

"Move!" Ashley yelled.

I moved my feet a few inches at a time trying to walk without falling on my face. Ashley chuckled at my wobble, but I was determined to follow her orders.

"Out the door!" she demanded. Ashley kicked the door open. I wobbled out the door, outside into the parking lot.

Ashley violently reached into my pants pocket and grabbed my car keys. Then she popped open the trunk.

"Get in!" she ordered.

I hesitated.

"Get in, I said!" she yelled, poking me in the back with the gun.

I bent my knees to lower myself into the trunk. Ashley waited until my body was all the way in, when suddenly a loud crash and screeching tires startled us both. Ashley turned her head toward the street, "Right on time," she said smiling.

"Good job, John-John," Ashley lauded, before slamming the trunk shut.

SEVENTEEN

Kandi

"GO, GO, GO!" The head of security shouted to the driver. We bobbed and weaved through the winding streets of the industrial park. The driver was having a hard time navigating the large limo through the tight curves. The tires screeched as they rubbed against the pavement. We held on for dear life as the back of the limo became airborne and crashed back down against the concrete.

"Turn right here, then left, and go straight ahead!" Eric fearlessly shouted out another set of directions to the driver. He was trying to save his daughter and I was trying to save my young mentee, America's future. The news van sped behind us. Inside of it were more guards and enough firing equipment to start a revolution.

"There's Jonathan's car!" I shouted, as I looked in the distance.

"And Ashley's car!" Eric blared out.

The limo hopped another curb entering the parking lot of A.V. Manufacturing, and came to a sudden halt. We held on tight as the force from the stop violently pulled our bodies toward the front of the limo. The security guards jumped out of the limo and van and headed for the door, all four of them with their weapons drawn.

Mitch and Eric tried to follow suit, but the head of the armed infiltration team pushed them back, "It's too dangerous, sir. STAY HERE!"

CLASH! One of the guards used the butt of his weapon to break the thick glass door. There was just enough room for the guard to reach in and flip the tumble lock. Once the door was opened, the first guard entered, as the other three stood waiting for the signal. Once the coast was clear, the guard motioned to the others, and one by one the brave armed guards disappeared into the massive dark building.

Eric, my crew, and I just stood in the parking lot dumbfounded, praying to God that the event would have a happy ending. For a moment, the earth stood still. The wind stopped blowing and birds stopped chirping. The doors to the limo lay wide open and the sound of the roaring engine was no longer noticed. All we could hear was the clear, crisp sound of a gun. CLICK!

"Don't you move," I heard a woman's voice say. "All of you turn around slowly."

We followed the directions of the crazed woman's voice and turned to face Ashley. Her eyes were wide and wild. I noticed the blood spots on her blouse and feared the worst for Jonathan.

"It's nice to see all of you again," Ashley said with an evil grin plastered on her face.

"Honey please..." Eric pleaded. He tried to take a step toward Ashley.

"HONEY?" Ashley angrily pointed the gun in Eric's direction, and he stepped back.

"Now I'm your honey. You never cared about me! All you cared about was work, work, work. When mom went away, it was actually your turn to put up with me, and all you did was push me to the side. You even let them have the Memo!"

Ashley turned and pointed the gun at me and my crew.

"Oh yeah," Ashley said, sucking her teeth. "You let the crew have it, Daddy!"

"I AM YOUR DAUGHTER! I'm your flesh and blood, and you let these clowns have the Memo. They enjoyed the success that I should have had. You let me fail, Daddy. I failed in front of the whole world because of YOOOUUUU!

Eric begged, "Ashley, I didn't mean..."

"Shut up, old man!" Ashley said to her father. "I handled it myself, and look Daddy I finally did something right."

Kim pleaded, "Please, Ashley…"

"SHUT UP, I SAID!" Ashley screamed. "Now, Daddy, I don't even want the book anymore."

"What do you want, Ashley? Just tell us," Leon jumped in.

Ashley looked at Leon as if he had three heads. "Do you have any kids Leon?" Ashley asked. Leon looked confused. Ashley walked closer to him. She swung her hand in the air and the gun's handle came crashing down across Leon's forehead. Leon fell to the ground with a thud "You bastard, do you have any kids!" Ashley yelled.

"No, no!" Leon yelled holding his head moaning in agony.

"I thought you would say that."

Ashley pulled the trigger hitting Leon in the chest. Kim and I screamed, as Leon's body bounced from the force.

The sound of the gun shots startled the driver. He looked in his mirror and saw the woman with the gun. He hit the gas and sped off in fear. The large vehicle fleeing the scene caused a distraction, and Ashley turned firing at the fleeing limo.

"MOM!" I heard a girl scream. Ashley turned to face Victoria, but not before Leon shouted, "GET DOWN!!!"

We all hit the ground, as Leon pulled out a small firearm from his waistband. *BOOM!! BOOM!! BOOM!!* Leon fired at Ashley, hitting her. Ashley fell to the ground, letting out a loud, piercing scream that seemed to last forever.

I crawled to Leon and lifted his shirt to search for the wound, instead there was a large black bulletproof vest protecting his body.

"Leon, where did you get this?" I asked, still shaking, but glad he was okay.

Leon replied, somewhat in a daze, "I grabbed it when the guards left me in the news van. I snatched the gun too."

Kim and I helped Leon get up, while Mitch and Eric tried to revive Ashley. Victoria screamed and cried frantically as she watched them try to revive her mother, but she got quiet once Leon approached. "I'm a doctor," he said. "Let me help." Leon bent to resuscitate Ashley, but he locked eyes with Victoria. It was something about her eyes that seemed so familiar. The eyes that he stared into had once belonged to his grandmother. The secrets that he kept in college were now exposed and before him stood his own flesh and blood.

ONE YEAR LATER

EIGHTEEN

Kandi

I slowly opened my eyes and my surroundings started to become clearer to me. I was in dream land but now it was back to reality. The sun shined into the windows and blinded me for a moment. I threw my arm in front of my face and with squinted eyes, I pierced through the window to view our location.

"Wake your butt up!" Kim yelled throwing her pillow up to the middle row. The hard foam pillow slammed against my head. I grabbed her pillow and tucked it under my butt, "This hard thing needs some softeners, I said smiling, acting like I was pushing out gas from my back side.

"Get off my pillow!" Kim yelled from the back of the car.

"You tossed this brick up here," I said laughing.

It felt good to laugh, because it had been a while since I was in a good mood, any of us for that matter. The last year had been tough. With the help of the police chief and the news reporter we were able to cover up the shooting, but no matter how hard we tried, there were always leaks. Every now and again there would be a reporter sniffing around. We ignored it, but the pressure was on.

We were all emotional wrecks, we had watched a friend die all over again. Before it was in a car crash, but this time I watched as she lay in her father's arms. Ashley was gone forever, but her father's guilt lived on. Eric would never be able to forgive himself for being such a bad father, but he was taking great strides to make sure that his daughter's death was not in vain.

Eric helped us to form an underground corporation that would secretly seek out young students, grooming them to become important fixtures in government, education, the business world, media, sports, and entertainment. We were building a program to create and mold the world's next leaders. Each student, with the help of recently recruited public figures and the lessons of *The Confidential Memo*, would navigate through the glass ceilings and red tape of corporate America and into powerful positions. After many years and intense training, the recruits would unite and initiate a series of international events that would result in better opportunities for the lower and middle classes.

During the Civil Rights Movement, the FBI established the Ghetto Informant Program in which members divulged sensitive information about the leaders of the Movement, in efforts to destroy the advancement of others. Our members were just the opposite; they were in place to help level the playing fields for all races, cultures, creeds, and financial statuses. We decided to call our recruits the Boojee Informants.

Our car swirled around the winding road right past the "Welcome Freshmen" sign posted along the side of the road. I looked around and noticed that Mitch, Leon, Kim, and Jonathan were all smiles. A car passed in the other lane as we barreled down the highway.

"Hey!" Leon yelled. He rolled down the passenger window. The wind came bursting through the car.

"Hey!" he yelled again as he pounded on the gas to catch up with the car. The college student turned to face Leon, wondering why he tried to flag her down.

"It's not her," Leon mumbled to himself. "I thought that was Victoria."

We all remained silent; there was nothing for us to say in that moment. Leon rolled the window back up. His face was expressionless as he guided us through the cornfields back to our old alma mater.

THE CONFIDENTIAL MEMO

Introduction

    To become a star employee, you have got to learn how to play the game. Corporate games are nothing like basketball, volleyball, soccer, or any other game that we used to play as children. In those games, it is strictly about athletic ability. Players put aside their presumptions and prejudices and the team with the most strength and ability wins fair and square. Unfortunately the corporate world is filled with presumptions, prejudices, and big burley shoulders with big hairy chips on them. Your enemies will smile in your face, take you to lunch, and even ask about your private life. Despite popular belief, the smartest person usually doesn't win the corporate game. The person that is perceived as being polished, knowledgeable, and most of all, likable will walk away with the trophy.

    The corporate game closely resembles the game of chess. In order to win, the player must use thought, strategy, and pre-planning. The player must be able to analyze the long and short run effects of his or her moves. A great player sees the bigger picture and understands that he or she may lose a few pieces during the game, but the sacrifice is well worth the championship. The player also puts on a game face that doesn't allow the opponent to read his or her thoughts or emotions, as they can reveal hints of the next calculated move.

    I will discuss ten sections of the original *Confidential Memo*. My crew and I have tailored each section for your generation. These are not hard lessons to learn. They are just tips that you should add to your everyday routine and even incorporate into your lifestyle.

The ten sections that I will discuss are:

I. Perception is Reality
II. Watch Out for That Bus
III. Stay Away from the Buts
IV. Earn Respect
V. Work Hard
VI. Don't Snap
VII. Lessons
VIII. Politics
IX. Achieve the Look
X. The Future

I

Perception Is Reality

One of the hardest concepts to learn in corporate America is that perception is reality. You may be doing a great job and working extremely hard, but if your boss thinks you are a slacker, guess what? You're a slacker. Most people think they can conquer this concept by letting their work speak for them. The fact is that in corporate America, you need to do much more than that. Your personality, work ethic, and employee relations are additional attributes that will shape other employees and your boss's perception of you. Listed below are methods that you can use to be perceived as an outstanding employee:

1. Always, I Mean Always, Smile - I have had a problem with this one since the beginning of my career. I grew up on the South Side of Chicago and in my part of town you don't walk around smiley. That's the fastest way to get GOT! A smiling face means clown, goofy, loser, and most of all, easy target. So to avoid the extra nonsense, most people walk the streets with a more aggressive facial expression, and after awhile it just becomes a habit. A straight face or snarl doesn't necessarily mean that a person is unhappy or evil. The mean mug is just a form of protection. For all I know, they can be thinking about pink cotton candy, a chocolate bunny, and a tall glass of milk.

I carried this habit with me into the workforce and I couldn't understand why people thought that I was mean and unapproachable. Finally, someone was brave enough to break through my tough exterior and explain it to me. My straight face and flat tone of voice scared people. Even though I was nice and extremely accommodating, my outward appearance caused people to think exactly the opposite. So I tried something different. I smiled at people as they passed me in the hall, I took the bass out of my voice and inserted just enough helium to keep myself from getting a sore throat when I talked to co-workers. I also laughed at stupid lame jokes and I even bobbed my head up and down and made noises like, "mmm hmmm," when people explained different tasks to me. All of a sudden, I went from being cold and unapproachable to being one of the most likable people in the office. What a difference a smile makes.

2. Face Time – It is such a bad idea to pack up and leave at 5 p.m. on the dot when you are in the early stages of your career. Some of the jerks that you work with are going to expect you to be the grunt worker and slave for twelve hours of the day. They want you to forget about family, personal time, and even bathroom breaks- you're theirs, and theirs for the taking.

Nobody in their right mind wants to go through that, so you have to find a happy medium. Stick around your desk for an additional 30 to 45 minutes after quitting time or until after the first couple of people break for the door. This may sound painful, but the sight of your smiling face will make that jerk watching you feel like you are hard at work, dedicated to doing their job, and willing to pay your dues to climb the corporate ladder. I know that sticking around the office is the last thing that you want to do, but there is an upside to this rule. Nobody said that you had to sit at your desk for an additional 30 minutes and actually do work. Heck no! Pay your bills, surf the Internet, and make dinner plans with your friends.

3. Work on the Weekends- Pick a day out of a month to respond to an email on a weekend. These responses don't have to be long, drawn-out emails. It could be the assignment that you completed

Thursday before your Monday deadline. Hold off on giving the report to your boss on Thursday and instead email it to your boss early Saturday or Sunday morning. The document sent to your boss with the weekend time stamp will have a much bigger impact than turning it in early during the workweek. Your boss will have no choice but to assume that you were up all weekend burning the midnight oil. As a matter of fact, if you turn it in too early you may find yourself with an additional assignment.

4. Self Starter – The people that you work with want you to do way more than just work. They want you to be a problem solver, a consultant, and an asset to the team.

How do I do that? you ask.

Easy.

Create effortless tasks for yourself.

No matter how busy your office is, there are always going to be moments when you are idle. These moments may include the week of a national holiday when everybody takes off to travel, when all of management attends a required all day meeting, or just at noon when most of the office is out to lunch. Use those moments to uncover and solve the small issues that everyone else ignores. For example, you log into your company's database to retrieve a customer's account balance. While in the database you notice that the customer's address is incorrect. Even though changing the address was not part of your assignment, you take the steps to contact your support staff to make sure the address is corrected in the system. You even take this to the next level by checking and correcting all of the customer addresses that are in your unit's portfolio.

This is what corporate America calls a self-starter; you take on issues and solve them without direction. Taking on these small issues will not add much to your workload, or require much additional time, but I'll bet you your bottom dollar that your office will think you are the best thing since sliced bread.

Please understand that moderation is the key for this lesson to work. If you do anything too often in corporate America, people will begin to expect you to do it all the time. Keep these additional assignments and "weekend" work days as pleasant surprises.

5. Take Credit, Work Your Work - Toot your horn, ring your bell, and sound your siren! Do whatever you have to do to let your boss know about all of your hard work. Go sit in your boss' office and give him a rundown of the week's activities, or send an encrypted email stating your accomplishments. For example,

"Hey team,

After lots of hard work, the monitoring system is updated and ready to go! Feel free to contact me if you have any questions.

Thanks."

If you don't toot your own horn, one of the other backstabbers hovering over your cubicle will gladly take credit for it. After all, what's the point of staying late and creating projects for yourself if no one knows that you are doing it?

6. Attend Happy Hour - When Friday afternoon finally rolls around and the clock hits 4:59, I am sure that mingling with co-workers is the furthest thing from your mind, but before you change into your walking shoes and warm up your bus pass, please think twice about attending the office happy hour. Your ability to be social is very important. After a few drinks, you will be surprised to hear the types of important information that just so happened to skip over your cubicle.

Constantly saying 'no' to "happy hour" sends the signal to other employees that you think that you're better than them and their stinky little job too. You can only be invited into the clique by rubbing elbows with the members, and if you are not a part of the clique, then get ready for the mean girls. Do yourself a favor and attend the after-hour events to avoid being ostracized.

Unacceptable excuses for not attending happy hour include:

- I don't like those people: You're lucky if you like your co-workers, so join the rest of the world and get over it.
- I don't drink: that's fine, just make sure you have some kind of beverage in your hand. You don't want your co-workers to feel uncomfortable.
- I don't like that restaurant or eat that type of food: live outside of your box and see lesson seven.

7. Learn the Menu - Just because you have never eaten a certain type of cuisine before doesn't mean that everybody has to know about it. Just fake it until you make it.

Ask for the name of the restaurant in advance and head straight to the Internet. This will allow you to view the menu in advance, read reviews, and get meal suggestions from past patrons.

Researching the chosen eatery online has worked for me when dining at restaurants that have menus written in languages other than English, especially when the meal descriptions are not provided. Usually, I can at least find a description or picture of the entrée to help with my decision.

If you don't know the name of the dish, don't try to say it. I have been embarrassed a few times when I mispronounced the name of some favorite Italian entree. I have just learned to point and say, "I'll have the chicken". If you don't have enough time, follow the lead of one of your co-workers, " Umm Tom, that sounds good. I think I may go with that as well."

You should also be familiar with the etiquette of different types of restaurants. An example is the Tapas bar. At this type of restaurant the servings are very small and you are to order many dishes to share with your party. I was recently at an event and one of my co-workers ate directly off the serving plate refusing to share with the rest of the party. I'm sure you can imagine the whispers.

8. Travel the World - Be familiar with current issues, different cultures, sports, plays, art, travel, and music. This will allow you to participate in conversations with your co-workers during happy hour and lunch dates. This will also help you during the office celebration of different ethnic holidays. There will be plenty of occasions when a co-worker will bring in an ethnic dessert to celebrate his or her favorite holiday. You don't want to be the one to look at the funny shaped donut and ask, "What's that?" Take it from me; your co-workers will have a field day.

9. Speak the Language - Just when you thought that your grandfather was the hardest person to understand, you entered into the work world and now you're surrounded by people who only express themselves by using sports analogies and lame clichés. If you want to know what the heck they are talking about, please see the following chart.

Cliché	Translation
Drink the Kool-Aid.	Just shut up and go with the flow.
Let me wrap my arms around this.	I need time to understand this, 'cause I don't even know what you're talking about.
Is this fully baked?	Does this include everything?
You are over-engineering this.	You are thinking way too hard.
Let's get a temperature check.	Let's stop and ask everyone else what they think about this.
We need to run this up the Flag Pole.	We need to make sure that our managers approve of this.
Just something to add to your Tool Box.	This training won't be helpful, but just listen anyway.
We need to do a Road Show.	We'll do presentations for the different departments to explain the new procedure.
The Writing is on The Wall.	Look at the signs. It should be clear what will happen next.
Do some word-smithing.	Rewrite this to make it sound better.

10. Leave Your Mark on Conference Calls - Never, ever, ever be silent on a conference call. You have to say something. Most conference call leaders will do a role call and ask for everyone on the phone to identify themselves. They know you're on the line and if you just listen quietly and take notes, your fellow co-workers are going to think that you are disinterested and not engaged.

Laugh out loud at the stupid joke that your boss makes or ask a question. If you agree with the speaker say, "umm hum", "I agree", "that's a great point". If you disagree, give your point of view, but preface it with a compliment. People need to hear your voice; if they don't, they will assume the worse.

11. Keep a Clean Desk - It is very important that you are organized and demonstrate the ability to mange your time while in the workplace, but in a fast-paced and sometimes overwhelming environment, these habits can become hard to sustain. So until you find the time to pull yourself together, make sure that you keep up the illusion that you are organized.

At the very least, leave a clean desk every night, even if it means throwing a stack of papers into a desk drawer and slamming that boy shut. It doesn't matter if you know exactly how to locate specific data on your desk that is hidden under the piles of policy guidelines and weekly newsletters. Nor does it matter if you have never misplaced sensitive paperwork. If your boss or co-workers see that you have a disheveled desk they will perceive you as being unorganized, no matter if it is true or not.

II
Watch Out For That Bus

No matter how much your boss wants you and your co-workers to act as a team, this job enables people to clothe themselves, feed their families, and make the interest-only payments on their maxed out credit cards (MESSAGE!). When the mess hits the fan, your co-workers are going to look out for themselves. If you don't cover your butt, you will be the sorry loser left behind to catch the blame. Listed below are a few methods that will keep you from being thrown under the bus.

1. Set Expectations - In many organizations you not only have to answer to your immediate boss, but you are also responsible for producing information or reports for more senior co-workers and various departments. This usually leads to heavy workloads with extremely demanding and sometimes unrealistic deadlines. The key to successfully juggling these frustrating tasks is to manage both your time and your co-workers expectations. Tell your co-workers exactly when they can expect you to complete their request. For small projects, keep your turnaround time between 24 and 48 hours; for larger projects, keep your turnaround time within the week.

2. Under Promise and Over Deliver - When giving a response to a co-worker that requires a hard date, leave yourself a one-half to a full day's cushion for unforeseen issues. The magic rule in this section is to never over-promise. You will leave a much better impression if you turn around a report on Monday that you promised to have on Tuesday.

3. Predict the Future - Probe co-workers to see why they need reports to detect if you have a showstopper on your hands. Showstoppers are additional steps or processes that need to take place prior to the completion of a project. These showstoppers can usually hold up processes and cause workers to miss deadlines. Be sure to complete these first. You don't want to be the reason why a process was not completed even if you received the information just 40 minutes ago.

Try to read the body language of your requester. If they seem annoyed by your turnaround time you may want to push them to the top of the pile or begin to manage them and their expectations through email documentation.

If the status of a project changes because of a major directional shift please make sure to communicate this to the original requester. Let them know exactly why their report was pushed back and establish a new timeframe in which they can expect the report. Be sure that the new timeframe does not exceed more than two days from the original promised date. If push comes to shove, prepare to stay at work an additional few hours to complete their request.

4. Clear Up All Assumptions - A lot of positions these days require the employee to use subjective thinking to make a decision. These decisions could be something as small as deleting a paragraph when editing a draft of a document. The problem with subjectivity is that your response to this type of issue is influenced by personal experiences that may include seniority, culture, and gender. Because of these differences your subjective decision may be different from others. Make sure that you erase the doubts of your judgmental co-worker by taking extra time to explain and discuss why you made your subjective decisions. This will open the doors of communication between you and your co-worker, which may allow for both of you to learn something new.

5. Email Leaves a Permanent Trail - Emails are a permanent paper trail and because of this some co-workers will try to avoid responding to emails by calling you. After you hang up the phone just send them an email that sums up the key points of the conversation. The email should begin with, "Per our conversation"...

6. Managing Needy Stevie - There will be those co-workers who think they are the only person that you work for or they believe that everything can be done "real quick." This person will typically ruin your day by calling your desk every few hours and blowing up your email. You have to be careful with this person because their high maintenance attitude has historically gotten them a VIP seat in your boss's complaint chair. If given the chance, this person would blab to the whole office about how much you suck as an employee. The only way to handle this person is to document, document, document.

For conversation purposes, we will call this co-worker Needy Stevie. Whenever Stevie asks you to complete a project be sure to send a detailed response by email. This email allows you to have evidence of the agreed upon turnaround date. The email should also explain your current workload and the additional work that their request may require. This will allow Stevie to see that you are just not pulling a date out of your behind, but that you are actually working as hard as you can to meet all expectations.

You may also be able to pro-actively handle Needy Stevie by forwarding him a pipeline report (See V. Hard Work, #3). Make sure to update this chart weekly and send it to your whole team. This will keep you from singling out Stevie and will also allow him to see that you are not just sitting at your desk waiting for him to assign you work, but you are indeed working with a number of other employees. If Stevie continues with his madness, approach your boss about the situation and remember to use your happy voice.

7. Trust No One!- Everybody is out to save their own behind and, when they need to, your co-workers will rat you out and use your long lunch breaks as a bargaining tool to get you out of the way. Nobody is your friend! Keep your business to yourself and slander your co-workers on your personal time. When you are at work, just act as if you love everybody.

8. Always Compete - Work is a competition. Always stay in the race or you will see people pass you by. Never get comfortable with your achievements, because someone is always waiting to take your place. Be aware of your co-workers' work ethics and performance, and make sure that you continue to rank accordingly.

9. Don't Talk in the Elevator - You never know who knows who. Just keep your mouth shut until it's safe.

III
Stay Away From the BUTs

Have you ever heard the saying, "It only takes one bad apple to spoil the bunch?" Well this saying holds true in corporate America along with many other circumstances in life. For some reason it seems that most people only remember negativity and no matter how great of an employee someone is, people will always find a "but..." For instance, Tameka is a good employee, **but** she takes way too many personal calls, or Mike is the best writer we have, **but** he's always late. The best way to stay at the top of the performance ladder is to minimize the number of buts that people can add on to the same sentence with your name as the proper noun. Also, if you annoy your employer enough, these buts will be added to your performance review and will be used as easy excuses to place you on probation and terminate you (because once you go on probation there is no coming back). Additionally your employer can contest your unemployment insurance due to buts. Oh yeah, they will take it there.

Remember:

1. Proofread - Always proofread your work and check your grammar. Live by the rule of double and triple checking. Your boss does not see your misspellings as simple mistakes, he sees you as illiterate.

2. Consistency - You want your boss to trust you and your work. In order for that to happen you must consistently produce excellent results.

3. Get You're Butt Off The Phone - I know how hard it is to ignore a phone call from your best buddy, but keep the personal phone calls to a minimum. Also, stay away from personal conversations with befriended co-workers. Trust me when I say that everyone is listening to you and they try to listen even harder when you whisper. This also pertains to paying bills over the phone. Make sure that you step away from your desk to handle your business by phone, or do it during your lunch break.

4. 60 Minutes - Everybody gets one hour for lunch. What makes you think that people are not going to notice your constant hour and fifteen minutes.

5. Attitude - No matter how much everybody smiles and says good morning, the truth is we would all rather be rolling around in our beds. Your bad attitude, lip smacking, eye rolling, ignoring of ringing phones, and refusal to respond to emails are just P-ing everybody off. I hope you know that they are documenting every move you make.

6. Be On Time! - Need I say more?

7. Internet - Be cautious of your unauthorized Internet usage. No matter how quickly you try to click and minimize the screen upon the sound of footsteps, it's very obvious that you were checking your fantasy football roster.

8. Don't Call in Sick - Your co-workers are depending on you to perform your job on a daily basis. When you call in sick you are interrupting the workflow, screwing with deadlines, and demonstrating irresponsibility. Only call in sick when you are actually sick. If this doesn't work for you at least cough a few times the day before your mysterious absence.

IV

Earn Respect

In the beginning of your career, no matter what your title is, you are the grunt worker. You have little to no experience and have everything to prove. You are the one that has to do the stupid low-skilled tasks, such as making charts, sending emails, and preparing countless revisions of the same assignment. Recognize it and make peace with it. You must be humble, open-minded, and pleasant at all times. You will be working with people who have been performing their job for 20 years and no matter if you like them or not, you have to find something to learn from them whether it be positive or negative. Sometimes your co-workers may try to treat you like a kid, but you have to earn respect and reiterate that you are a team member. Below are a few suggestions on how you can earn respect and work your way out of kid status and into the land of working equality.

1. Do it Their Way - When you hand someone a completed assignment, the first thing that they will do is race to find mistakes and suggest small annoying changes that are not material, but may better suit their personal preferences. Take notes and figure out their hot buttons. Consistently incorporate their nitpicky preferences in future assignments. For example, my boss always wanted me to create some sort of chart, no matter how simple the anaylsis was. Sometimes I felt that I was completing an exercise out of an Excel "How To" book instead of working at a prestigious institution. I took a deep breath and consistently implemented his suggestions into my work. Eventually his commentary went from extremely irritating to nonexistent.

2. Have an Opinion - Don't be afraid to show people that you have an opinion about a work issue. If someone asks if you like the new workflow process, don't be afraid to tell them how you feel about it. If you feel negatively about the process, be sure to do some word smithing and back your opinion up with examples. At the end of your statement show your undying love for the team by commenting on how you will help to solve the issue.

If you don't know how you feel about the topic at hand, say something to the effect of, "I haven't worked with the system long enough to have an opinion."

3. Participate - Here we go again, kids! You may have heard this one over one million times before, but speak up when in an open forum and participate in group exercises.

If you know that you will be involved in a discussion pertaining to a certain topic, pick up a book or use the Internet to quickly research the topic. This will help you to formulate questions, make small talk, have an opinion, and participate in the discussion.

4. Confidence - As a new employee with limited experience it can be difficult to exude confidence. But no matter what, you have to show people that you are confident in your abilities because if you don't, nobody else will. Here are some different ways to show your co-workers that you are confident without being cocky.

- Don't act like the youngest employee. If someone calls you, "baby girl" or "baby boy," you're headed in the wrong direction.

- Make eye contact, walk with your head up, shake hands, and make small talk with people. Ask people about their weekend and the pictures on their desk. In return, don't be afraid to tell people about your weekend. Of course you should only tell the clean version, keep the rest to yourself.

- Speak in a tone that is loud and clear. When you first meet people you should have an introduction prepared that tells who you are, the area that you work in, your manager, and how long you have been with the company. Example: "Hello, my name is Brittany. I work in Finance with Jim Conway, and I've been on his team for the past six months."

- Once again, participate and ask questions.

5. Be Aware of the Gray Hair - People in the workplace only seem to respond to people that look older or have big wig titles such as Director and Senior Vice President. Just because a co-worker has a more senior title or aged appearance does not mean that they are more qualified than you, the associate. They could be from another department or just new to the company.

From my experiences, if you are wrinkle free and still have a full head of hair, it is hard to get people to even respond to you. You are going to have to work past this, but I have found a few techniques that have worked for me.

If you, the youthful spring chicken, and an older co-worker are leading a meeting with a client, you are bound to run into this issue. Before the meeting, speak with your silver haired co-worker about the situation and form a plan. Once the client speaks, he or she will probably lock eyes with the elder. Have your co-worker look directly at you when this happens. This will remind the client that they should be focusing on you and not the crypt keeper.

When you can, use your co-worker's title or appearance to your advantage. When you need to close a deal, bring Santa along with you. The prospective client will feel important and believe that their business is important to your organization.

When dealing with an annoying employee who refuses to respond to your emails, just simply send another email to the employee. Attach the long chain of unanswered emails, but this time CC your senior team member or their boss. You will be surprised at how quickly the unresponsive employee will pull themselves away from their unauthorized Internet use to respond to you, the analyst.

6. Choose Your Battles - Sometimes you have to lose the battle to win the war. Do not take anything in corporate America personally. Nobody owes you anything and in the beginning of your career you will have to eat crow. You ain't running nothing, so don't try to. If you come in the workplace with airs and continuously try to prove a point, you will find yourself in the fetal position, waving a white flag.

V
Work Hard

Don't think that you are just going to walk in there, pull a few tricks from under your sleeve, and have the world handed to you. No, boo! You need to work hard.

1. Put Your Foot in it - There is no such thing as a draft. Whenever somebody asks to view a draft of your work, get ready for the criticism. Your boss is going to critique your work as if it was a final copy. Do yourself a favor and put your all into your work the first time around. This will minimize your boss's negative judgment of your work.

2. Pay Attention to Detail - The little stuff matters. Your boss will notice the spaces between your paragraphs, the missing dollar sign, and the number decimal places in your Excel worksheet. Make sure that your work is consistent. For example, if you mention housing costs of $512.13 on page five other references to these costs should remain the same. Do not site housing cost of 512.00, or $512.1 on pages six and seven.

3. Over Communicate - Build a working relationship with your boss that creates total transparency. Send a weekly pipeline report to your boss that explains exactly what you plan to accomplish down to the smallest detail. This Excel based chart should state what you are currently working on, the assigned date, who assigned it, the due date of each project and additional comments on your progress. This will allow your boss to get a feel for your workload as well as help to build trust between the two of you.

4. Be Proactive - Nobody should have to tell you to do anything. You should figure out what to do next. You should follow up on the email that you sent the day before yesterday, and if you get a "no" the first time, ask about the options available to you and just get the job done.

5. Read, Read, Read - The answer that you are looking for is only five steps away. Read and research before you open your big mouth. The only questions that you should be asking are the ones that will clarify what you already know.

6. Take Ownership - I know, this crap is not in your job description, but because your eyes have glanced at the work, it is now your full responsibility to treat the assignment as if it was yours to begin with. If you don't, you'll find yourself taking full responsibility for all of the mistakes that you overlooked.

VI
Don't Snap!

I know you feel it. Your heart is starting to beat faster and your palms are beginning to sweat, and if you aim just right, you could bounce your coffee mug right off the top of a dude's nose. But wait! Take a moment to breath and think. Don't snap!

1. Think Before You Hit Reply - There will be times when someone will send you a bogus email that will make you want to slap the coffee breath out of their mouth! If the email questions your ability to do your job properly, you will have no choice but to respond. In your response make sure that you only state the facts because your feelings are irrelevant. Nothing is personal in business and any emotional references will only dilute your message. Before you send the email take a break and cool off. Once you are back to normal re-read your response to see if you went off the deep end at any point. Send your response once you make your changes.

2. Never Let Them See You Sweat - Don't get emotional while you are at work. Your outburst or comments will only add fuel to the rumor mill. Not to mention that your co-workers will immediately judge you. Is she happy here? Is he difficult to work with?

3. Send Emails That They Can't Respond To - As a young employee it can be very difficult to assert yourself and get a more senior co-worker to honor a request of yours. The best way for you to handle this type of situation is to send an email in which your more senior co-worker can't give you a negative response. First you have to stroke their ego, tell them the request, and then mention how their help will benefit the team. For example,

"Tom,

It is my understanding that you have worked on the Thomas account for the past couple of years and it is clear that you have done an excellent job at managing the account. Since the account has been transferred into my name, I would like to request that we modify the customer agreement and I would greatly appreciate it if you would help me prepare for the conversation with the client. I am sure that you know the client the best and can offer great insights that can help our organization retain this customer. Lets meet at four p.m., if you are available.

Thank you so much for your help."

What can he say after reading that. If he says that he declines your request, he will look like a jerk rather than a team player.

4. Passive Aggressive - In corporate America it is completely improper to be direct and aggressive. If you want something done without people getting offended or gaining access to your private thoughts, you must approach and respond to situations in a passive aggressive manner.

Listed below are the most used passive aggressive statements in corporate America:

Passive Aggressive Statement	Translation
When you get a second, can you walk these down to legal. They need them in five minutes.	Take these to the legal department… now.
Wow, look at all of these files, you must be really busy.	Clean your desk, pig.
Maybe, if we make a few grammatical changes, the document will be easier to read.	Who taught you English?
It's been awhile since I've heard any report updates. Do you have them handy?	I bet your lazy behind didn't update the report! Let me see it.
I don't think I read that the last time I checked.	Naw dummy, you're wrong.
Is something going on? Are you OK? I noticed that you left early yesterday.	Oh, so you just get up and leave when you want to, huh.
I strongly encourage you to take the training.	Don't take it and see what happens.

If your boss asks you to do something, you have no choice but to say yes; while on the other hand, when co-workers ask you to do something, you can't just plainly say no. Listed below are some of the best passive aggressive ways to decline an annoying co-worker:

Passive Aggressive Statement	Translation
Sure, let me get settled and I'll get right to it.	I just walked in the door. Beat it!!!!!
I'll do my best.	You'll get to the assignment but I ain't promising jack!
I'll ask my boss if she has a problem with it.	Heeecck No!
I have a few things that I need to get off of my plate…	I'm busy, you'll get it tomorrow.

5. BS Sandwich - Another good way to be passive aggressive is to create a BS sandwich. A BS sandwich is when you have a negative comment between two compliments. Example, "Your presentation was very good, your charts were a little misleading, but I found the topic to be very interesting." BS! The point of the statement was to tell you that your charts were of embryo quality, but it would be completely improper for the speaker to just come out and say that.

VII
Lessons

Listed below are the top lessons that I learned in corporate America... the hard way:

1. Never Get Comfortable - No matter how much your boss likes you, or how much the company brags about its stability, there is always a chance of a lay-off, whether it be you or your manager, a company acquisition, or a change in your lifestyle such as children or marriage. Because of these factors you should always stay prepared. Take advantage of your company's tuition reimbursement program. Stay ahead of the game when it comes to education. Don't wait until your boss tells you that you need the advanced degree. By that time it is too late. Most people are afraid to use the reimbursement programs because of contractual clauses that may require them to stay with the company for a length of time after borrowing. Don't let this scare you. If negotiated properly, the next job will provide you with a signing bonus that will allow you to repay the tuition that you borrowed.

2. When to Leave
- As we all know, the chance of a merger or company acquisition is a reality. As a younger employee these types of events can open opportunities that never existed before. Usually people in

higher positions with inflated salaries run from these types of activities leaving you to hold down the fort in their absence. The new employer just may give you the benefit of the doubt and allow you to continue on with the new title. If you stick through the organizational changes of the merger the key rule is to sit down and shut up. Drink the Kool-Aid! There will be rough times, but just work through them. If you sit, complain, and constantly voice how much you hate the new owner you will soon be out of a job.

- Be aware of how your department fits into the company's financial statements. Your division has a better chance of survival after a merger or acquisition if your division participates in revenue generation. If your division is purely an expense that shrinks the bottom line…watch out!

- If you are afraid of the merger and want to leave the company, it is best to leave with the pack. As noted before, there is usually a higher-up that will be the first to move and will require people that he/she trust to help run the new business. If you can, jump on the bandwagon. You will probably get a bump in pay, and you will be used to the work culture. Also, if you decide to leave your company, do not tell anybody the name of the new organization that you will be working for until you get there. All it takes is one negative phone call for your new job to rescind their offer.

- Through conversations with your boss and the change in the corporate culture, you will know when things are coming to an end. Use your intuition. Don't wait until somebody has to actually tell you that things are not working out, because when they do decide to tell you, they are actually saying, "You're fired!" By then it's too late.

- Also, a lot of companies have a policy that, if you are doing poorly, they must put you on probation for a period of time. Take it from me, once you get on the probation list, it's time for you to start looking for another job. There is no coming back from probation, only unemployment.

3. Switching Companies Pays The Bills - If you are looking for a big pay raise you are not going to find it by making a lateral move or even accepting a promotion. The only thing that your current job will offer is the standard three to five percent annual increase. You'll find the 20% salary increase when you accept a position elsewhere.

4. The Definition of Blackballed - Do you remember the line in the movies, "You'll never work in this town again!" Well, kid, it's true. Be careful not to burn any bridges or screw up the job so badly that your boss and co-workers can't stand the sound of your name. Remember that the world is a very small place and all of the major players know each other in some capacity. People will talk and spread the word about your behavior, leaving you without a job and no hope of finding another.

5. Keep Your Business to Yourself - Your co-workers are always competing, so be careful of what you share with them. Don't gloat about making the decision to attend a master's degree program or a second shift working part-time at another institution. People will get jealous of these activities or use them as an additional way to criticize your work. Example: "I noticed that you made a few mistakes on the last report that you put together, are your classes getting in the way of work?"

6. Voting - No matter what your political views are, regulations and new policies can directly affect your career. Be sure to vote in government elections to help secure your interests. Never discuss politics, sex, or religion in the workplace.

7. Get Your Own - Look at your job as paid training on how to run your own company. At the end of the day, the company will make decisions that will affect your pocket, time, and happiness. The only way to have complete control over your life is to start your own business.

VIII
Politics

Let's face it, there will be times when you do your best, remain consistent, put in the extra time, and follow all the rules but the promotion that you know you deserve went to the fast-talking airhead, who just so happens to be the daughter of one of the company's top paying customers. It's a disappointing reality but sometimes it's about who you know and not what you know. This can be an unfair advantage for someone that did not grow up in an affluent neighborhood or whose parents did not work in a profession. Listed below are a few tips, besides the typical networking, on how you can build relationships in the workplace to increase your visibility within your organization.

1. Run Your Ideas Past People - There may be times when you're working on a deal and you come across one of those subjective decisions that we discussed earlier. After you have taken the time to prepare and research your argument, pick up the phone and call a seasoned employee. Explain the dilemma to the employee and ask for their advice. This will give them a chance to show off their expertise and even give them a sense of appreciation that someone finally recognized their hard work. Just by doing this you will have automatically gained a friend. Your new friend will also speak very highly of you when he or she converses with other seasoned employees.

2. Get in Good With the Secretary - The executive assistant knows everything from employee salaries to who is cheating on their wife, based on the number of hotel stays allocated on their monthly expense reports. Do not overlook this important jewel. Genuinely befriend the assistant and something good will come out of it.

3. Cross Department Lines - Just because you work in HR does not mean that you can't mingle with the people in the advertising department. The old saying goes that you can't judge a book by its cover and the same applies to the workplace. Smile and say 'hello' to people in the lunchroom, the elevator, and in the bathroom. Ask them what they do for the company. Typically, due to snotty co-workers, you may have been the only one to have actually acknowledged their presence. Because of this, you will be the first one that comes to mind if they have an opportunity to work with your department or just happen to know someone that may be of assistance to you.

4. Congratulate - Learn the craft of talking people up. If your boss asks you about your training you should tell him that the class was awesome and that the teacher was phenomenal. Speak about your business partners and co-workers in the same manner, especially when in front of their boss, even if they are committed to tap dancing on your last nerve. If someone does something to help you out, be sure to thank him or her for it and CC their boss on the email. Also, make sure that you return the favor.

5. Get A Mentor - Having a mentor is very important. Someone that has been in the industry for awhile can easily tell you the do's and don'ts, explain who's who, and even help you to navigate what can seem to be a very convoluted system. Within your first few years in corporate America you will be acting blindly, as the culture will be new to you. Sometimes it takes experience and wisdom that can be found in a mentor to make the right decision. A good mentor will be more prone to take a personal interest in your career and will work to help you achieve success. Most of the time it will be up to you to seek out a mentor who is compatible with your personality and remember that it is okay to have more then one.

6. Know When To Say 'Yes', Know When To Say 'No'- During your nine-hour day, you have to complete the work that is stated in your job description, answer the random questions that your co-workers have, help individuals with their projects, and work toward your goal of being promoted. The problem is that you can only be in one place at a time, and, hopefully you have only two hands. You must be able to manage your time and know when to say 'yes' or 'no', but before you open your mouth, check your ego and ask yourself the following:

- Who is asking (senior, subordinate, do I need them to like me)?
- What can I learn from this (waste of time, or exposure)?
- How much time will it take to complete (a few minutes or hours)?
- Can I say 'yes' and still delegate the tasks (give to the support staff)?
- Can you turn a 'no' into a 'yes' (Can I work on part of it, can the deadline be extended)?

Get creative and always try to give out more yes's than no's.

7. Make People Remember You - When you meet someone for the first time, make sure that they will remember you. Ask them about themselves so that you can quickly tap into their interest and most of all be yourself.

8. Be Visible - Don't hide in your cubicle. Get up and talk to people. Get involved in your company's diversity organizations and volunteer with the firm. Visit headquarters and work out of the offices for a day. You will be surprised by the powerful people that will begin to recognize your name, and when the opportunity arises I promise that they will think of you.

IX
Achieve the Look

In Corporate America people will judge you based on your first impression. As a new employee, it is essential that you understand how your wardrobe can affect your career.

1A. Women's Fashion (Put Some Clothes On)
- First of all, work is not a fashion show. In the beginning of your career, there is no need to break out the latest and greatest. Save it for the weekend. You'll be surprised at how quickly the secretary will compute the price of your new Gucci bag and resent you for being able to afford it. After all, she has been there longer than you and should be making more money, so how can you afford it, if she can't.

- Save the low-neck top, short skirt, platform heels, oversized earnings, and nail designs for the club. All it takes is for one person to see you speaking a little too closely to a male counterpart and before you know it, you will be labeled the office flirt or floozy. Not to mention that your exquisite nail art may have co-workers assume that you called off sick because you got a blister from sliding down the stripper pole.

- Dressing conservatively and neatly will always win against the fashion star. Until you have proven yourself and understand your company's culture, err on the side of conservatism. It would be a shame if a few baseless rumors got in the way of your success. I'm not saying that you should dress like a bum or wear over-sized clothing to hide your figure, but there is a way that you can still be conservative and cute.

Makeup
- Be sure to keep your face bright and clean. Do not overdo the makeup. Stick with tones that play off of your natural beauty. Stay away from the dark smoking eyes during the day and anything with glitter.

Hair
- There should be no pressure for you to wear your hair processed, natural, or in a weave or wig. Whatever style you choose, make sure you are comfortable. With comfort comes confidence. Your hair should be neat and away from your face. When I say neat, I mean an individual should be able to determine that there was an attempt for you to style your hair that morning.

- Some say that hair is a form of expression, but in the workplace nobody cares. Be conscious of the color and the length of your hair. The goal is to appear natural and you don't want to be confused with a drag queen. As long as you're not performing at the Grammys, you will fit in just fine with a weave that does not end at your butt.

1B. Men's Fashion
- Men, please make sure that your clothes fit you. Your pants should not hang below your waist and I should not able to see the outline of your belly button through the shirt that you accidently placed in the dryer.

Hair
- Make sure that your hair is neat and your face is shaven, clean, with no facial hair at all. There is no need for you to indirectly express messages of your depression through the follicles of your caveman mustache and beard.

- Early in your career you may want to stay away from extreme hair styles, such as Mohawks, mullets, and braids. Clean cut is the way to go. It will allow co-workers to focus on your fine abilities without being sidetracked by your appearance. Again, once you prove your abilities, have more control over your career and learn your company's culture, you can deviate as needed.

2. **Technology**
- We all love Social Media, but you must be careful of what you put into the universe because it can come back to haunt you. As an example, a manager gave our team all of the names of the candidates that were interviewing for a job opening in our department, mainly to see if we had worked with the individual before and could offer some insight on personality and work ethic. Sadly, a couple of employees typed a candidate's name into the computer and learned about his alcoholic tendencies and terrible potty mouth. Needless to say, he didn't make it past the first round interview.

- Be cautious of your ringtones while at work. It's already embarrassing when your cell phone rings and disturbs the whole sea of cubicles. Imagine how it would appear if your phone rings and sings "Let's get wasted".

3. **Tattoos** Cover them at all times.

X

The Future

Unlike the educational life that you've mastered, your corporate career does not come with a syllabus or a registration booklet to help you navigate your way to the finish line. You don't automatically get a counselor whose purpose is to help provide extra guidance when you need confirmation, feel confused, or plan on making a directional shift. You don't have a defined timeline or a curriculum that spells out how and when you will move from junior to senior. In corporate America all you have is yourself. You have to take control of your career, make your own timeline, and be aware of the pitfalls. Listed below are a few ways to help you clear away the debris of the workplace to reveal your own special path to the next level that YOU desire:

1. Tell Your Boss What You Want to Accomplish - For some strange reason people are afraid to actually tell their boss what they want to accomplish. You probably have a one-on-one with your boss on a quarterly basis. Most people dread these conversations or go into the meeting with the smile and nod routine, pretending that everything is all good. You should use these one-on-one meetings with your boss to your advantage. Before the meeting take the time to create a *reasonable* timeline for you to move into the next position. Have your boss comment on your timeline and work together to create benchmarks.

This is an easy way for you to create your own curriculum to guide you to the next stage, as well as provide a forum for you to clear up any misconceptions that you may have about any upward movement. The paper document that you and your boss have created will make each of you accountable for your actions, and if your boss doesn't hold up his or her end of the bargain, then you should begin your job search.

2. Work Outside Your Job Description - You have to be a jack of all trades. If you work with other teams or divisions to perform your tasks, take time to get an understanding of what they do. For example, learn how to read or even create their reports. This will allow you to catch mistakes and communicate results more effectively.

If you haven't noticed, in order to move to the next position you have to do the job that you want, before you get the title or paycheck. I know it's a sucky reality, but that's how it goes. If you worked with your boss to create a curriculum, then you will know exactly what you need to do to earn the qualifications for the desired position.

3. Always Ask For Feedback - Constantly ask your counterparts for feedback on any assignments that you have worked on and make sure to incorporate their suggestions in future projects and assignments. If you save copies of your work along with their feedback you should be able to prove that you have grown and improved in your performance.

4. Follow Through - Make sure that you complete tasks within a timely manner. When you are working a very demanding job, it can be very easy to forget about your co-workers' off-the-wall requests. To help you remember these tasks, jot down these requests as part of a daily 'To-Do List,' or record them in your electronic email as a reminder. Once a task is complete, mark it off of the list. Make sure to update your requester on your progress and be sure to alert him or her on the outcome. If you accidentally forget to complete a task, your requester may feel as though you blew him or her off, which will never result in a good outcome for you.

5. Numbers Don't Lie - In order to keep your job and move up in the company, you have to produce. People can like you all day long, but if you can't get the work done, then what is the point of you being there. At the end of the day, the numbers are what keep you in the game.

6. Accept the Challenge - Don't be scared to take on additional tasks. Show that you are a team player and that you have the ability to step outside of your position. This will allow you to gain additional experience and your boss will see you as more of an asset to the team. If you feel overwhelmed, see if you can negotiate for your boss to be more nimble on datelines or maybe even shift some work off of your plate. You will look worse if you turn down the offer.

Conclusion

I know, I know… there are a lot of rules to follow. In the beginning you may feel a little awkward interacting in the corporate world. It may feel like every move that you make has to be calculated or that you are a fake and not truly being yourself while at work. All of these are legitimate feelings, but after awhile you will find your happy medium. You will find a place that will allow you to be yourself, but still respond to situations as a champion corporate player. It just takes time and practice. Just like the game of chess, corporate America has nothing to do with athletic ability and team work. To win at the corporate game, the competing players must come with a strategy and the ability to use the clues in front of them to make sound decisions. The player must be able to see the bigger picture and understand that the goal is to win. Now that you have all the tools… Game On!!!!